An Anatomy of Musical Criticism

By Alan Walker

A Study in Musical Analysis

(EDITOR) *Frédéric Chopin:
profiles of the man and the musician*

ALAN WALKER

An Anatomy of
Musical Criticism

BARRIE AND ROCKLIFF
LONDON

"The value of a principle is the number of things it will explain."

EMERSON

ACKNOWLEDGEMENTS

My thanks are due to Christopher Headington, who read the typescript; to Balint Vazsonyi, who read the proofs; and to Diana Slattery, who typed the script and helped me to deal with correspondence.   A. W.

CONTENTS

Preface   page xi

Part One   *A Solution in Search of a Problem*   1

Part Two   *Creative Principles*   11

Part Three   *A Theory of Unconscious Assimilation*   89

Conclusions   106

Bibliography   108

Index   110

Index to Music Examples   113

PREFACE

MY book is about musical criticism—its practice and its theory. I wrote it because I was intrigued by the challenge of this great subject.

The practice of criticism boils down to one thing: making value-judgements. The theory of criticism, therefore, boils down to one thing also: explaining them. If you formulate a theory of criticism, it is not enough to know that one work is a masterpiece and another is a mediocrity. You must also explain why they are different. It is on this issue that my book takes a stand.

There is a widespread belief, especially keen today, that music lacks principles. It is too often assumed that composers, performers, listeners and critics are drifting aimlessly through history on a tide of fashion which sometimes brings them together, sometimes keeps them apart. Composers are composing in one direction, for performers who may play in another, for listeners and critics who may respond in yet another. Whether or not music succeeds depends, apparently, upon *casual*, not causal factors.

I do not share this feeble philosophy; but I think I understand it. Musical styles change drastically from one generation to another. So do listeners' reactions. Faced with such extreme opposites as Mozart and Schoenberg, Beethoven and Stravinsky, one is hardly encouraged to postulate the existence of constant, creative principles which all these great masters have followed. Each seems to pursue his own arbitrary path. Yet I believe this to be an illusion. Masters do not write masterpieces by accident. Nor do we recognise them by accident. Far from being arbitrary, I believe that masterpieces unfold according to timeless, creative principles, that they would not be masterpieces unless they did, and that it is the chief function of any theory of musical criticism to tell us what these principles are. This is the task I have set myself, although the present book amounts to no more than a survey of the basic issues.

There have been at least three major attempts to place musical criticism on a sound theoretical basis. These were by Hadow (1892), Calvocoressi (1923) and Newman (1925). Newman, in particular, was obsessed with a life-long search for the principles of what he called "scientific" musical criticism. He maintained that musical criticism, if it was to succeed, must be raised from the level of a hit-or-miss affair to the level of scientific certainty. Calvocoressi and Hadow were no less scientific, although they did not use the term. The fact is, all three musicians wanted to give criticism some teeth. They tried to introduce *criteria* into criticism. A critic without *standards* was, to them, a soldier without weapons.

I think they were mistaken. It is a purpose of my book to show that, by the very nature of things, you cannot have critics with standards; you can only have *music* with standards which critics may observe. I think, too, that they were mistaken in an even greater respect. For them, a value-judgement was something you possessed only after you had *finished* the critical process—it was, so to speak, a prize that you won by careful, objective, intelligent effort. I regard this attitude as a major disaster for criticism. For me, a value-judgement is something you must possess *before* you can even *start* the critical process; a value-judgement is pre-conceptual; it comes across as part of the musical communication. Criticism, as I understand it, only explains something you already know on an intuitive level. This paradox is one of the central topics of my book. Meanwhile, to put my case in its most primitive terms: you need not prove that the *Eroica* symphony is a masterpiece before you can be certain that it is a masterpiece. The reason is simple: its mastery is self-evident.

Much more important to a theory of criticism is the question: why is it self-evident?

ALAN WALKER

Hampstead, N.W.3.
February 1966

Part One

A Solution in Search of a Problem

IN a sense, musical criticism has not yet begun. I do not mean that musicians cannot criticise. The problem is more subtle than that. Rather, they do not know how they criticise. Separating musical sheep from unmusical goats is basically an intuitive process. We sleepwalk our way through music observing, often with somnambulistic certainty, what is good and what is not. But we still know next to nothing about the way in which we do it. Perhaps, it may be objected, we do not need to; a theory about our musical reactions will not necessarily make us better critics. True; but the crucial function of theory is not to improve practice: it is to explain it. Its great task is to bring into sharp focus the principles behind musical communication.

"A Priori" Principles

It is often asserted that a theory of criticism based upon an acceptance of *a priori*[1] principles is doomed to failure. My book was written in the belief that such an assertion is almost certainly wrong. A masterpeice is not a matter of chance. Neither, for that matter, is a mediocrity. Both are symptomatic of deep, far-reaching principles; music's fate is sealed internally, as it were. When these principles function, you have a masterpiece; when they malfunction, you do not. A crystal dashed to the ground, breaks along its predetermined lines of cleavage. I believe there are "lines of cleavage" in music—definable principles which govern the way in which it

[1] I use the term *a priori* in its strictest logical sense, i.e. "from cause to effect". I do *not* use the term as a substitute for "arbitrary", a connotation often loosely given to it by some musical theorists.

3

behaves. Such principles are *a priori* because they are there before the beginning; we cannot conceive of a masterpiece which does not express them. They are the immutable laws to which all genius gives unconscious utterance.

Several important consequences flow from this view.

First: cutting across all musical barriers—light, serious, chamber, orchestral, vocal, etc.; cutting across all historical styles; cutting across all shades of opinion, all varieties of taste, there runs a simple line of division. On one side fall those works which express music's timeless, creative principles; on the other fall those which do not. The division is crucial. It is one of my deepest convictions that it splits off the world's best music from the world's worst.

Second: "taste" is not a tool of criticism but a symptom of people. Tastes change. A switch in taste must, logically, involve untruth. How can today's masterpieces become tomorrow's mediocrities? A masterpiece either is, or it is not. You cannot have it both ways.

Finally, there are no critics with principles. There are only works with principles. Criticism does not settle music's fate; it observes music's fate.[1] An important concept now emerges.

Creative Determinism

Music is autonomous; it develops according to its own laws. This is one of the axioms of musical aesthetics. Paradoxically, while there is wide agreement about this axiom, there is a curious reluctance to accept its consequences. These are threefold.

(1) A musical communication is complete; it refers to nothing outside itself. Mendelssohn was once asked the meaning of some of his *Songs without Words*. His reply summarises an entire philosophy.

> There is so much talk about music, and yet so little is said . . . Words seem to me so ambiguous, so vague, so easily misunderstood in comparison to genuine music . . . The thoughts expressed to me by music that I love are not too indefinite to be put into words, but on the contrary, too definite.[2]

---

[1] The story goes that a man once went to an exhibition of paintings. He walked round all the galleries paying particular attention to the old masters. As he left, an attendant said to him: "I hope you enjoyed our collection of paintings, sir". "Not bad", came the reply, "but I didn't like your old masters". The attendant paused. "With respect, sir", he said, "it isn't the old masters who are on trial here". There is no need to labour the parallel.

[2] Letter to Marc-André Souchay, 1842.

4

The *totally musical* nature of musical communication is something I want to stress. Music is non-conceptual. It neither requires nor demands an "explanation". It is a purely musical truth which can be comprehended on a purely musical level.

(2) If music is autonomous all our knowledge about it must flow out of our experience of it. I do not think it is sufficiently realised that there is no valid theoretical concept in the entire history of music which did not first emerge as an intuitive part of creative practice. Musical theory is always wise after the creative event:

> *Robert Craft:* "What is theory in musical composition?"
> *Stravinsky:* "Hindsight. It doesn't exist. There are compositions from which it is deduced. Or, if this isn't quite true, it has a by-product existence that is powerless to create or even to justify."[1]

(3) Unless you already understand music, a theory about how it works is beside the point. Knowledge without understanding is a curse of our age. I know this is heresy in some circles. The entire field of musical education, for example, is slanted towards the belief that the "way in" is through knowledge—theory, analysis, history, etc. Modern psychology, however, shows that this is really the "way out". A child might be said to "feel" that a certain woman was its mother and later come to a "knowledge" of this fact through mature reflection. Similarly a theory of music comes into its own by explaining, *post factum*, your musical experience to you; in the deepest sense, you cannot teach anybody anything he has not already experienced.

The philosophy I am expounding, creative determinism, leads inevitably to a definition of criticism. It is a definition that I shall follow rigorously throughout my book. *Criticism is the rationalisation of intuitive, musical experience.* I maintain that you cannot criticise anything of which you have no previous intuitive understanding, for your value-judgement *is already contained in* such understanding.[2] Nobody postpones responding to music until he has set it against a critical yardstick. We respond first, criticise last. This is my basic

[1] *Conversations with Igor Stravinsky*, by Igor Stravinsky and Robert Craft, p. 16, London, 1959.

[2] A point of view which rests on a sound philosophical and psychological foundation. One of Aristotle's maxims was that "the judgement resides in the observation", while the entire field of "Gestalt" psychology confirms over and over again that critical perception is an intuitive, not an intellectual, process.

5

objection to the so-called "scientific" approach to criticism. It encourages the notion that we do not know whether music is good or bad until we have subjected it to an "objective" test. But the whole point is that we *do* know. As soon as we have taken that first intuitive step towards a work, we know instinctively whether we are dealing with something trivial or something great. As for the "criticism" itself, this is merely a rationalisation of something we already know to be true on an intuitive level. The real dilemma facing most critics is not that they cannot recognise musical quality without yardsticks; it is that they can, but do not know *how* they can.[1]

If we follow to its logical conclusion the view that music develops according to its own principles, we shall quickly find ourselves on a collision course with the historians and the scholars. I did not plan this clash. It was inherent in the situation from the start. It arose, inevitably, the moment we began to pursue the consequences of such a fundamental assertion.

The notion that stylistic developments can be explained in terms of historical "pressures"—political, social, economic, etc.—the bread and butter of the history books, is misleading. The case against it is really very simple. There are no *successful* stylistic changes in music which are not, at the same time, artistically necessary. I find this fact impressive. If you wish to explain a musical event, you do not have to go outside music to do it. The history of music lies in music. The historical background against which music unfolds, I submit, plays a passive, not an active, role in music's development.

---

[1] Everybody searches for proof of mastery when they should, instead, be attempting to answer the question: *Why* is mastery self-evident? The argument has been put to me in private that I am making a false distinction between the two, that once you attempt to disclose causes of mastery you are at the same time putting forward an attempted proof of mastery. There is a difference, however, and it is of some importance, philosophically, to get it right. The two tasks have different aims. If you want to *prove* mastery (and I do not), you cannot take mastery for granted: this is the very quality you are trying to demonstrate and you can only do so with criteria which are themselves "proved". This has been the undoing of all "scientific" criticism; it results in a *petitio principii*, a begging of the question. If, on the other hand, you want to attempt to *explain* mastery, you are already taking this quality for granted; you are moving in after the event, as it were. As for the vexed question of what exactly constitutes "proof", modern philosophy does not provide us with an answer. C. E. M. Joad once stated the great limitation of proof rather wittily. "You cannot prove proof. In order to do so, you not only have to beg the question, but you also have to steal the answer."

6

That is to say, history merely offers an ever-changing series of alternatives—political, social, economic—through which music might, or might not, develop. The final choice is, I maintain, always musically, always creatively determined.[1]

Ernest Newman used to tell a story to illustrate this point. There was once a village idiot. Every day he used to visit his tiny local railway station and stand on the platform waving a flag. Promptly at noon, the big London-bound express would come thundering down the tracks and roar through the station with the village idiot waving it on. Having fulfilled this crucial duty, he would then depart until the next day, when the ritual would be repeated all over again. I find this analogy illuminating. The flow of creative events can be observed, but it cannot be controlled. What, then, is the role of criticism? We are sometimes told its role is to bestow value. I think this is a fallacy. Music's value is inherent. A poor work cannot survive for long, irrespective of the propaganda poured out on its behalf. By the same token, a good work cannot be permanently suppressed merely because critics do not at first comprehend it. Criticism is wasting its time when it attempts to control the flow of artistic creation. It will simply be swept away by the current.

In the light of the foregoing discussion, I should like to consider two aspects of critical practice which seem, to me, fallacious.

Methods of Comparison

I have never understood the high premium some critics attach to comparison. It has always seemed to me unreasonable to use one composer as a rod with which to beat another—for this is what "comparison" invariably amounts to. Work *A* is neither good nor bad because it is like work *B*. For the question then arises: why is work *B* considered *worthy* as a critical yardstick? Because it is like *C* which is also considered worthy? This is a charmed circle from

[1] Let me ask a simple question. Why does music die? I hold the view that it dies because it deserves to; it dies of natural causes. Musical scholarship has never properly acknowledged the difference between a work which is dead and one which has merely been knocked unconscious, so to speak, by an historical accident. You cannot revive a corpse. Music is not worthy of our attention simply because it has been buried by history. Our own culture has enough fatalities of its own without being saddled with those of the past. The critic has nothing to gain, and everything to lose, by following the detached, "scientific" methods of the musicologist. Criticism without artistic experience is impossible. Musicology without artistic experience is not only possible but probable.

which escape is difficult. Comparison brings us back to the all-important question: *Where* is music's value to be found? We are faced with a simple choice. Music's value is either *intrinsic*—in which case we shall know about it without our "yardsticks"; or it is *extrinsic*—in which case we shall arrive at the embarrassing conclusion that a great work of art is "great"through no fault of its own.

A particularly invidious form of comparison arises when critics appoint themselves to the rank of H.M. Customs and Excise officers whose function it is to spot composers smuggling contraband ideas from one work to another. To ask a composer if he has anything to declare while he is busily unrolling his music to public view is not a very intelligent question. Each act of composition is a declaration. If it did not owe something to somebody it would be intelligible to nobody. Elgar may be said to have "smuggled" the closing pages of *Tristan* into the final bars of his own Second Symphony. But the comparison is so obvious only a bad critic would make it; and only a fool would "devalue" the Elgar as a consequence. The likeness sheds no light whatsoever on the respective "value" of either work. The way pieces resemble each other is the least interesting thing about them. It is one of musical criticism's blind alleys.

Means versus *Ends*

Another is the way in which means are sometimes confused with ends. Means are precompositional; they are the concern of the composer. The critic's concern on the other hand, is the creative result. We put the cart before the horse when we censure a composer for employing a technique which, for one reason or another, we happen to dislike. By itself, a technique is neither good nor bad. It is incapable of receiving censure until it has fulfilled itself in a creative result.

Means are continually gaining the upper hand over ends in criticism. We are always being asked to admire a way of doing, not what is done. Witness the so-called "experimental masterpiece" which commentators are apt to refer to with monotonous regularity.[1] The fact is, there can be no such thing as an experimental masterpiece and it is a critical blunder to suppose that there can. An experiment is a *process*—a means towards an end; but a masterpiece *is* an end. For the rest, if the experiment comes off it is no longer

[1] I am thinking, among other works, of Sibelius's Fourth Symphony which has had this meaningless label tied to it for many years.

8

"experimental"; if it does not come off the result can hardly be a
"masterpiece".

Vox populi, vox Dei

I should now like to put forward a hypothesis which is of some
importance to my theory. *The potential aim of a great composer is to
communicate a universal, artistic truth.* In order to do so, he harnesses
principles in the service of his genius which prompt us to recognise
him. Immediately, certain objections arise. The evidence to support
such a hypothesis appears to be scanty. There are many works about
which there has never been universal agreement. It is this very
difficulty which makes a theory of criticism so elusive. So far, so
indisputable. Yet there are two reasons why I want to retain the
hypothesis. First: its operative word is "potential". I am not main-
taining that a great musical communication *is* universal, only that
it *may* become so. Second: overwhelming as such objections to it
may be, they only represent one side of the case. It is equally certain
that there are works about which no one disputes.

As for the question *"What* does music communicate?" no theory
of criticism can avoid it. Music is a vehicle for transferring a psychological situation. A listener who responds to music does so because he has unconsciously identified himself with it; it is not only
true *for* him, it is true *of* him as well.[1] No musician needs to be told
that the intuitive musical experience is a vehicle of truth far superior
to that of rational thought.

Why do masterpieces survive across the ages? Surely because
musicians are in general agreement that they *are* masterpieces.
Survival is a symptom of profound and widespread *recognition*.
Critics who cannot accept the notion that a universal response is
symptomatic of musical value often counter with the argument
that, if it were true, the most popular works would be the best—
a conclusion nobody accepts. Actually, popularity is not significant

[1] I develop this argument more fully at a later stage (see Part Three). Meanwhile,
let me add that the composer–listener relationship is one of the crucial problems of
musical criticism. It involves powerful unconscious factors, not all of which are
musical. We all know that there are some works where one may take any critical
stand and expect to meet with opposition from one quarter or another. We may
eventually come to suppose that many irreconcilable attitudes to music are not
founded on musical instinct at all, that they often involve strongly irrational
attitudes which are so deeply unconscious that it is beyond the power of anyone—
especially the individuals concerned—to overcome them.

because it increases music's value but because it *confirms* it. People who like the same piece prove the truth of one another's responses.

Vox populi, vox Dei is a dangerous doctrine to espouse in aesthetics. Yet it is equally dangerous to ignore it. The fact is, the *vox populi* is often a symptom of the *vox Dei*. To dismiss it arbitrarily is the essence of snobbery. To regard it as evidence is the beginning of understanding.

Ernest Newman posed the situation very well in his *A Musical Critic's Holiday*:

> I believe that if five hundred of the best and best-informed musical minds of the day—executants, critics and amateurs—were gathered together (leave out the composers because they are notoriously bad judges of each other) and asked which were the ten mature composers of the present decade who would be remembered and performed fifty years hence, there would not be three per cent of variation among them. Further, I believe that with a small percentage of variation, they would agree as to which works of each composer would survive him, and as to the relative future standing of the ten composers; and I believe that posterity would confirm their general verdict.

I agree entirely with the spirit of this passage. It emphasises a vital truth: mastery attracts recognition. Assuming that he gets a hearing, history shows that a master will never remain unrecognised for ever. How great a master he is, and how widespread the recognition accorded to him, these are subsidiary matters which should not deflect us from our main objective. A theory of criticism must explain what it is that constitutes the *difference* between the two extremes of mastery and mediocrity.

I have described the forward, creative sweep of musical development, a pre-determined artistic drive which carries composers, performers, critics and listeners before it, as "a solution in search of a problem". Perhaps an even truer description might be "a solution without a problem". Music is music; if we lived in an ideal world, that would be that. But nothing short of an Act of Parliament will stop us musicians intellectualising about it. The "problem" is how we do this.

Part Two

Creative Principles

W HY does a composition express itself through its *particular* medium? Why *that* medium? Why not another?

Immediately, we are face to face with a fundamental creative principle: *the identity of the idea with its medium.* In masterpieces, the limitations of idea and medium are one. A master's inner inspiration always adapts to his outer terms of reference. It does so in order to succeed as a communication. Individual instruments lay down individual limitations. If a composer ignores this fact, he is running risks. He cannot be certain that his creative aims will ever coincide with the musical results. Transfer a work bodily to another medium and the principle becomes self-evident. Let us look at some examples.

The first comes from Debussy's String Quartet in G minor. Great as it is, there are moments when the work poses unrealistic playing problems. Very occasionally, the music and the medium are at loggerheads. Observe the second movement, bars 64–67:

EX. I

This passage always generates a sense of crisis; it is difficult to render in time. The problem lies with the viola and cello. Their rhythmic difficulties are practically unsurmountable. Even where they are in telepathic communication, the only thing that prevents the structure tumbling about their ears is its brevity. The passage is inspired by keyboard technique. I think I can give a practical demonstration of this. Hear Ex. 1 played by any good string quartet. Then play it in this two-piano version:

EX. 2

The comparison will serve to remind you what rhythmic exactitude is all about. Two heads are here far better than four.

Among the very great works written for string quartet, Brahms's in A minor offers examples of music which is sporadically written against the medium. Consider the opening bars:[1]

EX. 3

The problematic viola part is so awkwardly conceived for the instrument that the flowing accompaniment it is so obviously intended to provide is invariably over-articulated, and even the best violists cannot prevent it leaping aggressively into the foreground where it

[1] See Hans Keller: "Principles of Composition", *The Score*, July 1960.

proves to be something of an unmusical nuisance to the other players. I must stress that this is criticism on the very highest level. Both the Debussy and the Brahms happen to be great works; but they are not great string quartets. The difference is important.

The concept I want to develop involves far more than the self-evident assertion that a flawless masterpiece "obeys" the "rules" of instrumentation. Indeed, a great composer is the first to discard these same rules when his inspiration is at stake. The fact is, something quite fundamental has taken place when a composer is truly at one with his medium. In some uncanny way he has unconsciously assimilated into his own musical character the characters of the instruments for which he so successfully composes. His conscious fluency in manipulating them is a symptom of the unconscious dominion he has so mysteriously acquired over them. That this "intuitive feel" for instruments (as opposed to mere knowledge about how they work) is a vital part of the creative process, is borne out by Carl Nielsen's observation made just after he had completed his Sixth Symphony: "It was as though I crept inside each instrument'.[1] I do not despise "mere knowledge" about how instruments work; at the same time, I do not underestimate the powers of the creative unconscious which is quite capable of pushing a Delius or an Elgar with somnambulistic certainty towards the goal of orchestral mastery without either of them having had a single, formal lesson in their lives.

Nowhere are the disastrous consequences of a split between music and medium more vividly revealed than in Beethoven's transcription for piano and orchestra of his Violin Concerto. Beethoven, in fact, has illustrated the principle for me. He undertook this transcription for Clementi who, having acquired the English publication rights of the Violin Concerto, imagined that a piano transcription would help promote its sales. Critical opinion is unanimous about the utter inferiority of the result. Beethoven shifts the violin part to the pianist's right hand *virtually unchanged*, supporting it with the most primitive of left-hand accompaniments. Moreover, he does not alter the orchestration by so much as a single note. The soaring lines

[1] It would be interesting to speculate on the reasons why certain composers unconsciously "identify" with certain instruments (thereby gaining complete control over them), and not with others. There is scope for musico-psychological research here.

of the sublimest music ever conceived for the violin are sapped of their tensions, and the piano's lack of sustaining power is cruelly exposed. Here is a typical example from the first movement:

EX. 4

It sounds like a musical-box. The passage would be much nearer the true spirit of the piano if the right hand forsook the violin's original pitch and dropped an octave. The following example, from the second movement, is even more depressing:

EX. 5

Again, the right hand "plays the violin". A wind instrument might have carried this line, but at this pace the piano certainly does not.

There remains only the question of Beethoven's motives. It is interesting to speculate why he permitted himself to send Clementi such a patently bad transcription. Perhaps he was in urgent need of money. I cannot believe he momentarily suspended his artistic conscience. I prefer to think he knew this transcription for the poor piece of work it really is. One explanation that would solve all the others is that it is not by Beethoven at all. But proof of this does not seem forthcoming. The transcription remains a museum-piece, one of the most baffling produced by any genius.

Stravinsky, as so often, has summarised the problem:

Robert Craft: "What is good instrumentation?"
Stravinsky: "When you are unaware that it *is* instrumentation."[1]

The distortion that results from performing a masterpiece through a medium for which it was not conceived, offers the clearest proof that a creative principle is operating in the original. Hindemith expresses it very well:

> Play some of the ... fugues from Bach's *Wohltemperiertes Klavier*, as string trio or string quartet pieces. You will have a queer and rather disagreeable sensation: compositions which you knew as being great, heavy and as emanating an impressive spiritual strength, have turned into pleasant miniatures ... the pieces have shrunk ... and their structural and spiritual relation to the original keyboard form has become that of a miniature mummified Incan head to its previous animate form. In our fugues we have reduced to almost nothing the heavy technical resistance that a player of polyphonic keyboard music has to overcome, since the string players have produced their isolated lines without noticeable effort.[2]

If the Beethoven transcription is a disaster from the standpoint of the principle of identity between idea and medium, Ravel's Piano Concerto for the Left Hand is an unmitigated success. The reason is obvious. To write a left hand concerto at all pre-supposes the recognition of a physical problem—and its solution. Ravel deliberately sets up a series of hurdles and then proceeds to scale them in public, so to speak. The *sight* of the performance and the *sound* of the music bring home the "idea-and-medium" principle in a unique way. Ravel composed the concerto for the Austrian pianist Paul Wittgenstein who had lost his right arm during the First World War. The "personality" of the music emerges so naturally from the problems of playing a keyboard with the left hand alone that the music sounds wrong when played with two hands. Although it may seem technically simpler with two hands, in actual fact two hands audibly drain the music of those tensions so surely created when the left hand plays it alone, tensions which are so essential in "placing" some of its notes on the right time-spot. Clifford Curzon, who

[1] *Conversations with Igor Stravinsky*, Igor Stravinsky and Robert Craft, p. 28, London, 1959.
[2] Paul Hindemith, *A Composer's World*, p. 122, paperback edition, Harvard, 1952.

17

has played the work many times, rejects the notion that the concerto loses nothing when played with two hands:

> Ravel has given the melodic line to the heavy "thumb" side of the hand where it receives a natural accentuation and singing quality. This is to be noticed especially in the last big cadenza. If, for practice, one picks out the melody notes with the *right* hand, it is surprising how much less well they sound than when they form the natural apex of the left-hand arpeggio figures. The roll of the arpeggio brings the melody note at the right moment musically with the right quality of tone . . . the very limitation from without has stimulated the composer—just as particular voices, etc., inspired other composers from time to time—to a remarkable achievement.[1]

EX. 6

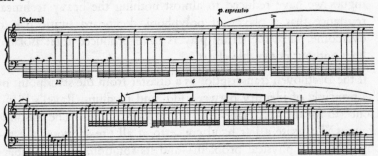

Occasionally, a great composer deliberately engineers a collision between idea and medium in order to enhance his musical intentions. The resulting friction becomes an integral part of the composition. Consider bars 36–41 of Chopin's C sharp minor Scherzo.

EX. 7

The abrupt appearance of the double octaves (*) is a crucial moment.

[1] From a letter to Norman Demuth dated 19 April 1946, printed in this author's *Ravel*, Master Musicians Series, p. 92, London, 1956.

In themselves, they are not difficult. They can be thrown off by any well-drilled virtuoso. Yet it is difficult to start them up to speed. The player needs a split-second delay in which to "change gear". No matter how well-oiled is his technique, the "lie" of the music encourages him to brake before the double octaves. A subtle hesitation is all that Chopin needs to bring out his meaning, for the octaves are a lead-in to a new phrase.

Let me give a similar example, again from Chopin. It illustrates this master's genius for using physical limitations creatively. In the Polonaise in A flat major (Op. 53) there occurs this highly characteristic passage:

EX. 8

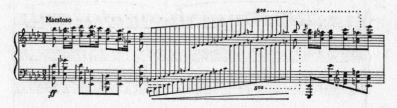

Not only is it technically difficult to play the second quaver of bar 3 up to speed: it is musically difficult, too. Chopin has tried to make it pianist-proof. The virtuoso has trouble stealing it for himself; it always steals the virtuoso. The implicit pause after the upward rushing scale is an unwritten, though essential, aspect of the music. Chopin makes it inevitable by virtue of the three and a half octave drop with which he confronts the left hand. Did anyone understand the piano better than Chopin?

There is a notorious passage in Wagner's *Parsifal* Prelude in which the music and the medium collide. Conductors quail at the mere mention of it. There are two problems. First: Wagner unfolds two time signatures simultaneously; the strings and brass are in $\frac{4}{4}$ while the woodwind is in $\frac{6}{4}$. The conductor cannot conduct both. Second: the overall time is so slow (it must be one of the slowest-moving pieces in the repertoire) *neither* signature can be conducted anyway without sub-dividing the crochet beats. The result of such sub-division is to aggravate still further the rhythmic problems of those players the conductor decides to abandon. Ex. 9 shows the difficulty involved:

21

22

The performance of this passage is always hazardous. When the two time signatures happen to coincide, this is as much due to luck as to any other factor. Now, I maintain that the sense of insecurity this passage generates within the orchestra is an essential part of the music. Wagner knew what he was doing. It would have been easy for him to compose the passage entirely in $\frac{4}{4}$ time (the instruments in $\frac{6}{4}$ time, after all, do nothing but add supplementary, accompanying chords which could easily be modified). The fact that Wagner chose to write against both the orchestra and the conductor, however, is explained by the "Holy Grail" theme (oboes, trumpets, violins) which becomes the one stable, rock-like element in an otherwise shifting amorphous texture. This passage is a masterpeice of music-psychological thinking which has led to the profoundest artistic consequences. Only a genius who knew how to write *for* the orchestra could so fruitfully have written *against* it.

There is an historical aspect to this principle which ought not to remain unobserved. Performers evolve; so do instruments. What is "impossible" today may well become possible tomorrow. The full potential of an instrument may only be revealed after it has un-folded across several generations; consequently, we should distin-guish between those ideas which genuinely extend their medium and those which actually come into conflict with it. Such a dis-tinction is not always easy to make and it must be admitted that even the most distinguished musicians have gone astray. Couperin considered that double thirds were impossible on the keyboard.[1] Yet later composers showed that this technique is an integral part of the keyboard. In Couperin's day it was merely dormant. Similarly, in his book on violin-playing, Leopold Mozart described violin harmonics as "trick work only fit for mummers at Carnival time". Nowadays, this "trick work" is a respectable aspect of the violin's character and one which lies comfortably within the field of its physical possibilities. One of the more celebrated cases of this kind of confusion arose over Tchaikovsky's Violin Concerto. The work has had an interesting history. It was written in less than two months

[1] *L'Art de toucher le clavecin*, complete works, Vol. 1, pp. 36 ff.

in 1878. Technically, it broke new ground. Tchaikovsky pushed back the physical boundaries of the violin in this concerto, uncovering a new side to its character. Leopold Auer, the distinguished Russian violinist, was offered the first performance. He turned down the work as "unplayable". Two years later, Adolf Brodsky proved him wrong by giving the first performance in Vienna. The "impossible" was possible after all. Nowadays, the concerto is one of the most widely played works in the violin repertory. So much for technical evolution. Snap judgements in this field can be fatal.

Beethoven's *Hammerklavier* Sonata rolls the historical and physical aspects of this principle into one. It still imposes severe instrumental limitations on even the greatest pianists. I say "still" because even now, 150 years after the event, few players are able to overcome them. The work's difficulties are of a curious kind. We know that Beethoven wrote the Sonata for posterity. He wanted to write a piece which "would make pianists work creatively, and which would still be played in fifty years' time". That he succeeded beyond his greatest expectations is now a matter of history. Like Tchaikovsky in his Violin Concerto, Beethoven here pushed back the physical boundaries of keyboard technique to a point never before reached. Unlike those of the Tchaikovsky Concerto, however, the technical problems the Sonata poses have not yet all been solved. In the notorious Fugue, especially, Beethoven goes out of his way not only to compose *against* the keyboard but to compose *beyond* it. The music lies somewhere in the instrument's future. I remain convinced that the *Hammerklavier* is not an intrinsically unpianistic work, as some critics maintain, but simply that the transcendental technique required to cope with its difficulties has not yet been evolved. But consider the following passage. It occurs at the end of the Fugue, at the end of the Sonata, at the end of more than forty minutes' gruelling technical punishment.

EX. 10

How is the left hand to descend, in less than a semiquaver, more than three octaves for the important tonic entry of the fugue subject, *and arrive on time?* No left hand known to me, even the greatest, has ever made it. I do not believe that Beethoven's made it, either. In fact, the fractional delay imposed on the left hand at this juncture is precisely what is needed to "point" the crucial fugue entry in the bass. Beethoven deliberately stages a fight between keyboard and music. The technical difficulty has been specially composed, so to speak, to bring out the musical meaning. It is a splendid illustration of the way in which a great master identifies a creative aim with a physical limitation. Should the pianist ever appear to whom the *Hammerklavier* presents absolutely no difficulties, I think his interpretation, paradoxically, would suffer.[1]

One of the most extreme cases I know of music which is deliberately composed *against* the medium is Webern's Piano Variations, Op. 27. It is possible to play this work in two ways. Contrast these two examples (Ex. 11(*a*) and (*b*)):

The first was written by Webern; the second was not. Yet, in both cases, the sounds are identical. The difference between these two versions lies in the way the notes are distributed between the hands. It leads to a built-in friction in the first example, an essential part of

[1] The chronic sense of friction that you get throughout the *Hammerklavier*, but especially in the Fugue is, in my view, an essential part of the music. It is highly instructive to compare Weingartner's orchestration of the Fugue with the original. In the orchestral version the music unfolds with ease, the last thing, in my view, that Beethoven wanted. On the other hand, the orchestration does make the counterpoint highly audible and also creates the possibility of hearing all the right notes at the right time . . . an impossible luxury in the original.

the texture, which is totally absent from the second. Any pianist who side-steps the work's physical problems in this way may still be playing the notes, but he is no longer playing the music.

I believe it was Sir Charles Stanford who advocated the "black and white" test. He maintained that all good music demonstrates its goodness by remaining good when played on the piano, irrespective of the medium for which it was originally written. This is palpable nonsense. It can so easily be proved false. There is no good musical reason why a choral or an orchestral masterpiece should happily transfer to the keyboard. One can imagine only too well what (say) Debussy's *Nocturnes* would sound like subjected to this treatment. Their orchestral and vocal colouring is an essential part of their communication. Of course, one understands what lay at the back of Stanford's mind. He wanted to emphasise the importance of real ideas, ideas which are so powerful they retain their *essence* no matter how you reproduce them. Yet once you are aware of the difference between the essence of an idea and its mode of reproduction, you are already criticising the musical result.

So much for my first principle. Instrumental limitations are there, *a priori*, before music is born. Music adapts itself to them in order to live. I regard this function as a *sine qua non* of creative mastery.

*   *   *

Let us now move closer to the creative process itself. Why does a composer choose the contrasting ideas of a masterpiece, *and no others*, to share the same framework? I think this question can lead to profound discoveries about the way in which music hangs together. Why, in fact, do particular themes *belong* to particular movements? Why do particular movements *belong* to particular works?

Masterpieces diversify unity. They grow from an all-embracing idea. If you wish to explain a work's contrasts, you will not get very far by confining yourself to the *manifest* music. You must listen for its *latent* unity. Behind music's contrasting themes lie the unitive forces that hold it together. A description of a work's contrasts will not tell you much more about them than you can hear for yourself, and it may tell you considerably less. But once you have grasped the underlying unity of a masterpiece, you understand its diversity at the same time. More to the point, you are in a position to demonstrate it.

I want to formulate the underlying principle like this. *All the contrasts in a masterpiece are foreground projections of a single, background idea.*[1] What evidence is there to suggest that this principle is true? Musical experience, as usual. There is a perceptible difference between works which hang together and works which do not. Moreover, there is an elementary experiment with which anyone can test my hypothesis. Try substituting themes from one masterpiece for those from another. The result may be chaos. But even where it is not, it will lack the masterly inevitability of the original. Where you lessen unity, you also lessen meaningful diversity. For the rest, where there is no unity to begin with, there remains nothing to diversify.

I am, then, concerned with explaining music's *manifest* contrasts by way of its *latent*, unifying drives. It seems to me that this approach offers some highly fruitful possibilities to musical criticism. One word of caution, however, concerning the manner in which I shall present this topic. My music examples will make the reader work. They carry the burden of my argument. They are there to be actively heard, not passively gazed at. Where they do not drive the reader back to the relevant score, they will drive him to and fro among themselves—that is, if he wishes to follow my argument which is addressed to his ears. I have, as a matter of course, deliberately compressed my "explanatory" text which, in the circumstances, would have been tautologous.

Let us begin by considering an elementary example of the unity of contrasting themes. In Mozart's C minor Piano Concerto (K.491) the soloist's first entry runs:

EX. 12

[1] This principle is demonstrated in detail in my analytical essay *Chopin and Musical Structure.**

First introduced by Heinrich Schenker, the foreground–background aspect of musical structure has since proved extraordinarily fruitful in musical analysis. It might be termed the "depth" aspect of a composition. At one time, "analysis" was simple description. Nowadays, it has almost become a reversal of the composing process. Real analysis, in fact, moves from foreground to background, from the level of contrast to the level of unity, seeking to explain the one in terms of the other.

* *Frédéric Chopin: profiles of the Man and the Musician* (ed. Alan Walker), London, 1966.

Compare this with the following example from the same work, an "episode" in the Larghetto:

EX. 13

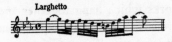

As contrasts, these two ideas are diverse enough. But once you really know them, really know the concerto from which they come, you experience their unity too. The latent force that they express I have formulated thus:

EX. 14

Far from being random shapes, Mozart's two themes are, in fact, different aspects of a single thought.

Let me give another example, equally simple, this time from Tchaikovsky. In his Fourth Symphony, two of the first movement's most sharply contrasted ideas run:

EX. 15

EX. 16

In the foreground, all is diversity. In the background, all is unity, for both themes spring from a common source. The basic idea which inspires them both is expressed as follows:

EX. 17

Nowhere is the unity of contrasts better illustrated than in Elgar's Violin Concerto. Two of its themes (from the first and second

28

movements) hang together so closely that they even make satisfactory counterpoint.

EX. 18

Telescoped in this fashion, these contrasts give the clearest proof
that they unfold over a common background.

Mozart's Piano Quartet in G minor (K.478) offers a similar
example. The kaleidoscopic variety of its contrasts has occasionally
misled commentators—even the most illustrious. Of all the themes
in the Quartet, one of Mozart's major masterpieces, none presents
a greater challenge to our theory of unity than the first and second
subjects of the great, opening Allegro.

EX. 19

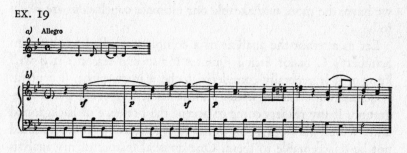

Analytically, these two contrasts are among the most mysterious
in all Mozart. We feel their unity (assuming we understand the
work), yet it is quite another matter to formulate it. Of the several
modes of demonstration which exist, I choose the simplest. Mozart
himself prepares the ground for me by transposing his first subject
into the relative major (bar 23; Ex. 20):

EX. 20

29

We now hear both themes as variations on the same basic idea. Like my previous Elgar example, Mozart's contrasts can be telescoped into one another:

EX. 21

Many questions now demand an answer. Is background unity audible? Does it hold good for *all* masterpieces? Are composers consciously aware of it, and if not, just how true is it? These, and other problems, I shall discuss. For the present, however, I want to postpone drawing any conclusions. I should simply like to multiply these observations about the unity of contrasts; the more evidence we have, the more unshakeable our ultimate conclusions are likely to be.

Let us attempt the analysis of a complete work. I have chosen Schubert's C major String Quintet for several reasons: it is well known, it is generally considered to be a masterpiece, it contains wide-ranging contrasts which present interesting problems of integration. If my readers come to accept the presence of background unity within the work, some of my final conclusions about it should not be unacceptable to them. One unusual feature of my analysis calls for explanation. I have deliberately ignored the *chronology* of Schubert's themes. I have allowed myself the freedom of moving in any direction, any distance, back and forth across the entire, impressive range of Schubert's ideas. There is an excellent reason for this. Schubert's thematic chronology enhances his themes' contrasts; this, after all, is why he chose it in the first place. Yet it is our present task to get behind the diversity. By avoiding a head-on collision with his ideas, so to speak, I hope to demonstrate more about their unity.

The Quintet's inspired, opening idea contains the shape of things to come:

EX. 22

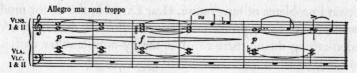

From its quasi-sequential continuation in the first cello (Ex. 23(a))
I have distilled the underlying, unitive drives (Ex. 23(b)). Hear first
Ex. 22, then listen to Ex. 23(a); Ex. 23(b) becomes self-evident:

EX. 23

Those who know the Quintet well, will recognise the connection
between the "distilled" background at Ex. 23(b) and the important
"episodical" theme in the second movement (Ex. 24):

EX. 24

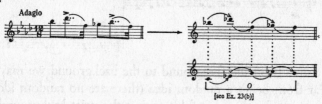

Again, and following the path of least resistance, the fourth movement's second subject expresses these same, all-pervading background forces.

EX. 25

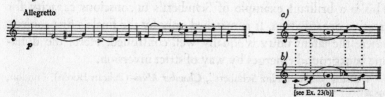

So, too, does the Scherzo's main idea which, at a first glance, offers awkward problems of integration. Hear Ex. 26 in the minor mode, however, and these problems diminish. Behind this aggressive, tension-raising theme there revolves the by-now-familiar unifying idea:

EX. 26

The first movement's second subject is one of the greatest themes in all Schubert. It is also one of the sharpest contrasts in the Quintet. It has been called "a serene, evening tune that floats in and out of G major and, at one memorable moment, is transfigured by a shaft of C major sunlight".[1] True or false, this is description, not analysis. The burning question is: How does this particular theme belong to this particular work?

EX. 27

If we move from the foreground to the background we may find out. Far from being a random idea (there are no random ideas in great music), the theme unfolds against the strict background of a retro-active O.

EX. 28

This is a brilliant example of Schubert's unconscious capacity for creative organisation. It is matched only by the finale's first subject, where the latent unity is equally well controlled. Here, the dynamic background emerges by way of strict inversion.

[1] William Mann, "Franz Schubert", *Chamber Music* (Pelican Books), London, 1957.

EX. 29

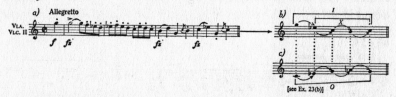

The integration of the first movement's codetta (and, consequently, the first movement's development section which is largely
based on the codetta's first figure) is achieved via bracket X in Ex.
29. Foreground and background are here remarkably close.

EX. 30

This development section has come in for some criticism. It contains a sequence of unprecedented length: the model is no less than
35 bars long and Schubert immediately copies out the entire passage
again—a major second lower (see bars 167–238). As an observation,
this is true. But as a criticism, it makes no sense, and for the simplest
of reasons: it is not based upon aural reality. The sequence is so long
it is inaudible. I invite anyone who has not yet heard the bad news
about this development to shut his score and to spot the "flaw"
aurally. I feel confident he will fail: and his failure will be a con-
firmation of Schubert's procedure.

There remains to consider what is, perhaps, the most violent
contrast in the Quintet; the Trio section of the third movement, the
Andante sostenuto. Even the most ardent Schubertians have been bewildered by it. Arthur Hutchings, in his excellent book on the composer, has remarked: "If all the repeats are played, as is customary,
this trio drags, and we ask whether this is novelty or originality
and, in any case, what is its relationship to the Scherzo? Why was
this form of contrast selected, which seems to belong to a dramatic
andante?"[1] The question is a fair one. But if we consider it in terms of
background unity it scarcely remains relevant. Like everything else
in this remarkable work, the Trio re-expresses as a foreground

[1] Arthur Hutchings, *Schubert*, Master Musicians Series, London, 1945.

contrast the same underlying progenitor, the same basic, inspirational idea.

EX. 31

[see Ex. 23(b)]

Its *Urlinie* (Ex. 31(*b*)) is a strict inversion of the Quintet's all-embracing, latent thought (Ex. 31(*c*)). Compare these examples with Exs. 29(*b*) and 29(*c*) where precisely the same background relationship operates (strict inversion); both sets of examples, in consequence, throw a mutual light on the two, respective foreground themes (Ex. 29(*a*) and Ex. 31(*a*)) from which they are derived. Indeed, these two themes, "unofficial" variations on one another, have far more in common than have many an "official" pair.

It is often asserted that you can discover connections *between* works just as easily as you can *within* works; therefore, the connections within works are not significant. I think that this conclusion is fallacious. By proving a unity between works, you do not thereby disprove the unity within them. To put this proposition another way: a relation between A and B is not nullified by revealing a relation between A and X. Do Brahms's *Variations on a Theme of Paganini* cease to express a unity simply because Liszt, Rachmaninoff, Blacher, and even Paganini himself composed variations on this same theme? It goes without saying that overt connections abound between these different sets of variations; yet each set, a different work in its own right, establishes its own internal unity. Let us distinguish between connections which are *causal* and those which are *casual*. The long arm of coincidence stretches everywhere throughout musical history. By all means analyse two works as one where they genuinely diversify a unity.[1] But where they do not,

[1] When Schumann reviewed the first edition of Schubert's Four Impromptus, Op. 142, he assumed on stylistic grounds that these pieces might, in fact, be a sonata. This view was later supported by Alfred Einstein. Their key-scheme, as well as their thematic content, makes such a view plausible. Here, I believe, is a clear case for analysing as *one* work a group of four "separate" pieces. See Deutsch's *Catalogue* of Schubert's works, No. 935.)

Brahms's Two Rhapsodies, Op. 79, also appear to represent such a broader

any attempt to fuse them will not stand for anything that is musically true. Doubtless one could force a connection between Palestrina's *Missa Brevis* and Gershwin's *I got Rhythm* if one were so minded. Yet the result would no more weaken our theory of unity than it would be a true explanation of one's real convictions about such "contrasts".

Actually, the unity of contrasting works, unlike the unity of contrasting themes, *is not a symptom of value*. It is with each *individual* composition that criticism is vitally concerned—the relationships which exist *inside* the boundaries of a composition rather than those which exist *outside* them. This crucial fact is the cornerstone on which all criticism rests. Nor does it cease to be true even when we restrict our observations to the output of a single composer. What are often referred to as the "finger-prints" of a composer's style—those recurring, life-long motifs which cut across his entire output, lending it consistency and continuity—are of interest to critics and scholars alike, yet they hardly reflect the "value" of each individual composition. One of the most familiar "finger-prints" in all Wagner is

EX. 32

which he re-composed many times and which recurs in works as diverse as *Rienzi* and *Götterdammerung*. Yet the intrinsic value of *Rienzi* and *Götterdammerung* is hardly affected by this relationship. If critics have not heard the one work, they are not thereby excluded from fully understanding the other. For the rest, the trouble with most so-called "identities" between works is not that they are not alike, but that they *are*. Contrasts, not identities, characterise true unities; contrasts, not identities, are the real challenge to analysis.

As for the Schubert Quintet, I do not even expect those who know it well to accept my analysis of it immediately, let alone those who do not know the work at all. Indeed, the better the musician knows

---

unity. Rudolph Reti has analysed them as one work in his book *The Thematic Process in Music* (pp. 139-50). Again, three of the last string quartets of Beethoven seem to diversify a unity (B flat major, Op. 130; C sharp minor, Op. 131; and A minor, Op. 132 respectively). They have been analysed as such several times. See Marion Scott's book on Beethoven, *Master Musicians Series*, pp. 265 ff.

the Quintet, the more likely is he unconsciously to cling to Schubert's contrasts in order to "save" them from dissolving into background anonymity. In any case, I am not trying to communicate its unity; Schubert does that. The chief task of analysis is to move in after the background unity has been communicated—and then expose it. Perhaps the reader has already observed aspects of my analysis that might expose unity more fully. If he can shoot me down with my own artillery, so much the better.

Let us extend our observations. Brahms's Second Symphony is particularly rich in thematic unity. It may provide some corroborative evidence.

The Second is the longest symphony Brahms wrote. Yet he completed it in the shortest time—just over two months. I do not think these two facts are unrelated. The work reveals all the symptoms of spontaneous creation. Of all Brahms's symphonies this one seems to me to have been conceived whole, rather than made whole. It has an impressive totality about it. While its contrasts are far-ranging, its unity is proportionately more powerful. Brahms was, in fact, the first great composer to unite his contrasts in public, as it were. His liking for openly proclaiming his themes' pedigree set in motion a trend which had repercussions down to Schoenberg and beyond.[1]

Once again, my analysis departs from the music's thematic chronology. By ranging freely across Brahms's contrasts, I hope to show more about their unity.

The Symphony begins:

EX. 33

In one form or another, this basic idea pervades the entire work. A step-wise curve, a falling fourth, a rising third; from these primitive elements Brahms builds one of his mightiest structures. Time and again, they turn up as part of the manifest content of the symphony. But they also play a deeper role. They express the background drive against which some of the work's extreme contrasts unfold.

[1] Schoenberg, "Brahms the Progressive", Style and Idea, London, 1951. See also p. 38.

EX. 34

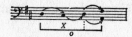

Take the third movement. Its opening, oboe melody seems to roam freely enough. In point of fact, however, it is pulled into shape by Ex. 35(b) operating by way of inversion.

EX. 35

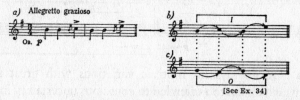

These same unitive forces flow beneath the fourth movement, holding together its contrasting first and second subjects.

EX. 36

Brahms's ability to evolve large, composite structures from tiny motifs was a milestone in the history of form.[1] Ex. 34(x) scatters its progeny far and wide. Here are just a few instances.

EX. 37

[1] Another was his development of the symphonic finale. In all four of his symphonies the finale is at least as weighty as the first movement, and in at least one case (the C minor Symphony) it is actually weightier. The only historical precedent is Beethoven's Ninth Symphony.

The Symphony's basic idea even invades such distant regions as these "transitional" bars in the slow movement:

EX. 38

Brahms here deploys his motivic variations with great skill. A technique which has too often led to conscious uncertainty in others, is used with unconscious certainty by him.

Schoenberg, a great admirer of Brahms, turned thematic unity into a cornerstone of his philosophy of music. He once vividly described unity in the following way:

> A real composer does not compose merely one or more themes, but a whole piece. In an apple tree's blossoms, even in the bud, the whole future apple is present in all its details—they have only to mature, to grow, to become the apple, the apple tree, and its power of reproduction. Similarly, a real composer's musical conception, like the physical, is one single act, comprising the totality of the product. The form in its outline, characteristics of tempo, dynamics, moods of the main and subordinate ideas, their relation, derivation, their contrasts and deviations—all these are there at once, though in embryonic state. The ultimate formulation of the melodies, themes, rhythms and many details will subsequently develop through the generative power of the germs.[1]

Our observations already go some way towards supporting Schoenberg's description of the composing process. Indeed, there is a surprising amount of agreement among composers generally about the initial *totality* of the creative act. Beethoven, for instance, once wrote that

> the fundamental idea never deserts me—it arises before me, grows—I see and hear [it] in all its extent and dimensions stand

[1] Essay, "Folkloristic Symphonies", *Style and Idea*, London, 1951.

before my mind like a cast, and there remains for me nothing but the labour of writing it down.[1]

While Ernest Newman, writing of Beethoven, touched on the same point:

> We have the conviction that his mind did not proceed from the particular to the whole, but began, in some curious way, with the whole and then worked back to the particular.[2]

Hindemith, perhaps, expressed it most clearly of all:

> We all know the impression of a very heavy flash of lightning in the night. Within a second's time we see a broad landscape, not only in its general outlines but with every detail. . . .
> Compositions must be conceived in the same way. If we cannot, in the flash of a single moment, see a composition in its entirety, with every pertinent detail in its proper place, we are not genuine creators . . . Not only will [the genuine creator] have the gift of seeing—illuminated in his mind's eye as if by a flash of lightning—a complete musical form (though its subsequent realization in a performance may take three hours or more); he will have the energy, persistence, and skill to bring this envisioned form into existence, so that even after months of work not one of its details will be lost or fail to fit into his photomental picture.[3]

Great contrasts, then, belong together because they were *born* together.

For another demonstration of the unity of contrasting themes I wish to turn to Tchaikovsky's Symphony No. 5 in E minor. The work unfolds about 45 minutes' music, about 45 minutes' tension-raising contrasts.[4]

No descriptive analysis fails to point out, in the name of unity,

[1] From a written conversation with Louis Schlösser.
[2] *The Unconscious Beethoven*, Ernest Newman, p. 120, London, 1927.
[3] Paul Hindemith, *A Composer's World*, p. 70, London, 1951.
[4] One day, when the history of *composition*, the history of musical *ideas* comes to be written (as opposed to the conventional, socially inspired histories of music), Tchaikovsky will emerge as a leading figure in the development of the contrast-potential of large-scale musical structure. See my analysis of his Symphony No. 4 in F minor (*A Study in Musical Analysis* pp. 116-26).

the "motto theme" (Ex. 39) with which the Symphony begins and which reappears in all four movements.

EX. 39

Yet, if this foreground tune were all that these movements had in common, the Symphony would be impoverished; indeed, it would not be a symphony. As usual, we must plunge beneath the surface for some answers. Ex. 40 distils from the "motto theme" a basic shape which is, I submit, the common background against which all future contrasts are composed.

EX. 40

Again, I shall put this proposition to a practical test. I shall range freely over the musical foreground in an attempt to enhance its latent background.

The first movement's first subject begins:

EX. 41

At first glance, the manifest notes appear to have no connection with the Symphony's introductory theme (Ex. 39). But as soon as we hear them in terms of the latent idea (Ex. 40) the family relationship leaps to the ear.

EX. 42

The first movement's ensuing transition section (bars 116 *et seq*) is a "new" theme in the dominant minor, not based, apparently, on anything previously heard.

EX. 43

Once more, we should think in terms of background, not foreground; we should listen for the latent ideas, not the manifest notes. Ex. 44 "condenses" the theme and reveals its derivation.

EX. 44

[Compare Ex. 40]

We begin to understand what Tchaikovsky meant when, discussing symphonic form on one occasion, he remarked: "The details can be manipulated as freely as one chooses *according to the natural development of the musical idea*" (my italics).[1] I should like to draw a corollary from Tchaikovsky's observation. All great music is variations; to compose is to diversify! In a masterpiece, no event will take place for which there is no precedent. Every direction the music follows is pre-determined by the "natural development" of the basic idea. We shall soon discover how far Tchaikovsky himself supports this notion. Some 15 minutes further into the future of the work there emerges the following theme, the second movement's second subject (bars 24 *et seq*.), a future which would be inconceivable without a past. Note its strict thematic organisation.

EX. 45

The subsequent, contrasting episode (bars 67 *et seq*.) presents a complex problem of integration—together with a complex solution.

[1] Letter to Nadejda von Meck, 1878. Tchaikovsky's reference to "the musical idea" (in the singular) is of significance in the present context.

EX. 46

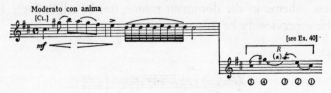

The theme, as we can hear, unrolls over the basic idea in retrograde motion.

The second movement's first subject, that long *cantabile* melody for
solo horn,

EX. 47

is symptomatic of the Symphony's endless foreground variety. Yet
even here, the latent idea moulds according to its own image the
very sweep of the melodic line. Ex. 48(*a*), the first four bars of the
theme, and Ex. 48(*b*), its subsequent continuation, show the latent
idea in masterly diffusion:

EX. 48

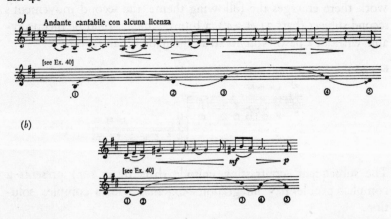

The third movement is a Waltz, one of the very few in the history
of symphony. Its chief motif:

EX. 49

is integrated by way of interversion and octave transposition among the notes of the basic idea (Ex. 50).

EX. 50

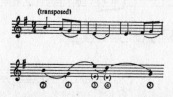

Tchaikovsky's successful incorporation of a Waltz into a large-scale symphonic structure, while not without precedent,[1] is a creative act of major importance. It ought not to remain unrecognised. From the symphonic point of view, the result could have been a disaster; yet it is a triumph. The dance-model has been fully sublimated; the waltz-elements completely digested. (I regard as a symptom of creative mastery the assimilation of weaker structures into stronger ones. This, as I understand it, is what *musical* history, as opposed to musical *history*, is about. You can no more dance to this Waltz than you can dance to the waltzes of Chopin. Tchaikovsky here finally clinches the claim of the symphony upon the waltz. Five years later, in the third movement of his *Pathétique* Symphony, he repeated the feat by clinching the claim of the symphony upon the waltz's opposite number—the march.)

It is an inescapable consequence of our theory of unity that there are no "free" passages in music—except bad ones. Indeed, it is a symptom of creative mastery that the "freer" the foreground seems, the stricter is the background against which it unfolds. We should not underestimate the powers of thematic organisation possessed by the musical unconscious. Certainly, in this Symphony's finale, Tchaikovsky reveals a superb gift for unconscious tightrope walking. The Allegro vivace's two chief contrasting ideas are so far-flung, only an intuitive genius could pick his way from one to the other and maintain his balance.

[1] See, for example, Berlioz's *Fantastic Symphony* (1831).

43

(a)

(b)

What, we may well ask, have these two themes in common with one another, let alone with the rest of the Symphony? Ex. 52 demonstrates the connection. It shows that the background urges of both themes are complementary aspects of the work's all-embracing, latent idea. Ex. 52(a) revolves around the notes 1–3–2 permutated from the basic idea by way of octave transposition of the first degree and interversion of the second and third. Ex. 52(b) flowers from the notes 1–3–4–5 of the basic idea with octave transposition of the first and the fifth. Telescope these backgrounds and they lock together like pre-selected pieces of a jigsaw puzzle (Ex. 52(c)).

EX. 52

Tchaikovsky, we may be sure, was blissfully unaware of this com-

44

plex integration. He would no more deliberately compute his thematic organisation in this fashion than a pedestrian, guided only by a desire to get to the other side, would work out a geometrical progression before crossing the road. Tchaikovsky was guided only by his creative conscience. Yet for that reason, this sleepwalking genius remains a fascinating study for all musical analysts.

Some musicians might disagree. They might maintain that what is not consciously intended can hardly become part of a meaningful, artistic communication. This is a naïve point of view. It is misleading to suppose that what is conscious is meaningful, while what is unconscious is not. Indeed, what is unconscious is, by its nature, dynamic and far-reaching in its creative consequences; all the more likely to be meaningful, then. Composers themselves have made penetrating self-observations which provide a great deal of evidence in favour of unconscious musical organisation.[1] Moreover, from the listening end, we observe far more than we know. We hear unconsciously, too. The notion that the complex demonstrations of unity sometimes revealed by analysis cannot possibly be heard unconsciously receives no support from depth psychology. What cannot be grasped unconsciously, cannot be grasped.

For my final illustration of the unity of contrasting themes I want to turn to Beethoven's Eighth Symphony, in F major.

The work begins:

EX. 53

Enough has already been written about this idea on a superficially descriptive level. Beethoven builds up almost the whole of the first movement's development section from this motif, as most commentators are quick to point out. But this merely describes what everyone hears anyway. On a deeper analytical level, much yet remains to be explained. For the motif is, in fact, the key to the unity of the entire symphony. The family of contrasts which forms the work can trace back its pedigree to this one, inspired source.

[1] See, for instance, *The Musical Underworld*, p. 81. See also my earlier book, *A Study in Musical Analysis*.

EX. 54

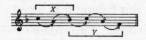

Not only does the *Allegretto*'s first subject secretly betray its origins *via* a strictly inverted X:

EX. 55

but its contrasting second subject openly proclaims them revolving, as it does, round a background of both X and Y.

EX. 56

One is reminded of Schubert's penetrating remark that "Beethoven's genius is the result of his superb coolness under the fire of his creative fantasy".

The Minuet raises a number of interesting problems. Why a minuet? Beethoven himself had made the form redundant by replacing it with the scherzo. Yet he chose to include a minuet in this late work, the only occasion he ever did so in any of his symphonies. The fact has not yet ceased to inspire commentary. However, once we look at the Minuet in terms of the total structure of the Symphony, its function is obvious. There is no slow movement. The only possible contender for this title is the *Allegretto* which does not move nearly slowly enough. Had Beethoven composed a scherzo instead of a minuet, the Eighth Symphony would be the only great one in musical history with three fast movements, and it would be proportionately less interesting, less great. As it is, the Minuet allows the Symphony to express a far wider range of contrasts; at the same time, it presents a stiff, analytic challenge. How does this movement hang together with the rest of the work?

Its two leading themes are:

at the beginning of the Minuet, and

EX. 58

at the beginning of the Trio. Plunge beneath their surfaces, and you find their inner currents determined by the same latent force: both themes flow out of Y in reversion.

EX. 59

As we have seen, a corollory of any theory of unity is that all great composing is the art of writing variations. While "variation form" has become a *genre* in its own right, it remains true that even if it had not, the technique of varying must perforce have emerged. Indeed, variation technique might then be more widely recognised for the universal thing that it is: variations not so described tend to be dismissed as "accidental". All of which brings us to a consideration of the Finale's opening theme, which gets off to this flying start:

EX. 60

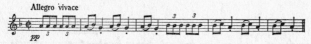

Where have we heard the theme before? It previously appeared, in simpler guise, towards the end of the first movement's exposition.

EX. 61

Both themes, in fact, have their roots in the very opening of the symphony; they express X by way of retrograde inversion.

So far, I have said nothing about the first movement's second subject. It presents a ticklish problem of integration. Everybody talks about its initial appearance in the "wrong" key of the sub-mediant major. But this only emphasises its individuality. What we wish to discover is the way it expresses the basic idea.

EX. 63

The simple answer is that it does so by way of the subtlest rhythmic diversification. Rewrite Ex. 63 thus:

EX. 64

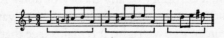

and its connection with the symphony's initial idea (see Ex. 53) becomes primitively clear.

The only facet of the initial idea that has not yet characterised any of the work's contrasting themes is the interval of the fifth (Z). It plays a role in the formulation of the last movement's second subject as, for that matter, do X and Y.

EX. 65

Like the key of the first movement's second object, the "unexpected" key in which the theme begins (mediant minor) has called forth much comment. It is not uninstructive to observe that the keys of both these themes stand in an exact "polar" relationship to the home tonic:

EX. 66

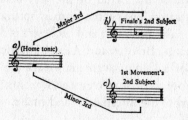

and that the interval of a minor third is the initial melodic interval with which the Symphony began.[1]

It is a corollory of our theory of unity (one which I expressed another way on p. 43) that where you have an unprecedented event in a musical structure that structure is correspondingly weak; an unprecedented event must, *ipso facto*, create discontinuity. There is no difficulty in finding examples to support this notion. Consider the off-stage recording of the nightingale in Respighi's *The Pines of Rome*. However "beautiful" it may or may not sound as pure bird-song, there is no real musical *raison d'être* for it. It does not diversify the work's basic idea at all (indeed, it would be a miracle if it did; we should be obliged to attribute to the bird in question a creative foresight of a most unusual order!) By contrast, the "birds" in Beethoven's *Pastorale* Symphony are much more musical; their calls are motivically inspired—as an analysis of the Symphony would soon show. In short, the Beethoven discloses ideas in contrast; the Respighi, ideas in conflict. There are many similar examples.

A study of the full score of Chopin's *Andante Spianato and Grand Polonaise* reveals that the Andante Spianato has nothing whatever to do with the Polonaise. Chopin composed the Andante Spianato some two or three years after the Polonaise. He appears to have nailed the two pieces together somewhat hurriedly for a performance in Paris. The lack of any intrinsic unity between them is made

[1] The connection between key-distribution and melodic motifs is nowhere better illustrated than in Brahms's Third Symphony. The key-distribution of the finale's exposition is F, A flat minor, F and C. Compare this sequence with the Symphony's opening idea:

Ex. 67

to sound even cruder by virtue of the fact that only the Grand Polonaise is orchestrated. The switch from a "spianato"[1] piano solo to an exuberant polonaise for piano and orchestra is difficult to accept.[2]

In 1853 Schumann, Brahms and Albert Dietrich collaborated in the composition of a four-movement sonata for the violinist Joachim. Dietrich wrote the first movement, Brahms wrote the scherzo, and Schumann wrote the intermezzo and finale.

EX. 68

The music is not without historical interest—but it is hardly a sonata. The movements are not binding on one another; for obvious reasons, the underlying unity is simply not there. The stylistic clashes are so violent that Joachim guessed the identity of each composer after a single run-through. Brahms's scherzo is the only movement one ever hears nowadays. By itself, it makes a

---

[1] Literally "smooth", "calm".

[2] When carried to extremes, dis-unity leads to the phenomenon of laughter music. One of the reasons we laugh at Ibert's *Divertissement* is that it does not hang together. Its contrasts are preposterous. It deliberately attempts to integrate such an immense variety of styles that unconscious confusion explodes into mirth. What we cannot accept unconsciously we cannot take seriously. This is corroborated by the experience of listening to "difficult" music. The laughter of the man in the street when confronted with modern works he fails to understand is well known. The unconscious background eludes him. The point about real laughter music is that it has no background; it is all foreground. Perhaps the most striking case of dis-unity is Mozart's *A Musical Joke* (K.522) which deliberately exploits this psychological situation.

splendid piece. In the context of the "sonata", though, it is hardly convincing.

An early version (1869) of Tchaikovsky's Fantasy-Overture *Romeo and Juliet* exhibits, among other things, an introduction that has no connection with the rest of the work.

EX. 69

Even though these bars return to form part of the coda, the lack of any real connection with the other themes is apparent. We may be sure that this was one of the reasons which prompted Tchaikovsy to revise the work. The later version (1880) not only has a different introduction but this introduction is fully integrated on both the manifest and latent levels of the work. Here is the familiar revision.

EX. 70

which returns to dominate the development and pulls the structure together.

Another striking illustration of Tchaikovsky's "unity-awareness" can be found in his Violin Concerto. Tchaikovsky only hit upon the idea of writing the present middle movement of the Concerto (the Canzonetta) as an afterthought. The original middle movement, an Andante, was rejected shortly after the Concerto was given its private, preliminary run-through. We need not regret the loss of that movement (which later turned up as a Meditation for violin and piano, Op. 42, No. 1). But it is not without interest to ask why Tchaikovsky felt it necessary to substitute another one. The answer lies in the music itself. The substituted Canzonetta makes a far better contrast than the rejected Meditation; indeed, it is difficult to see how the Meditation "belonged" to the rest of the work in the first place—which doubtless prompted Tchaikovsky to remove it. Genius is full of such "afterthoughts"—a regular feature of the creative process.

★   ★   ★

An important aspect of contrasts yet remains to be considered. The question: "Why do contrasting themes hang together?" prompts another. "Why cannot we successfully change the *chronology* of a masterpiece's themes? Why is one thematic chronology good and another bad?" A theory of unity cannot help us here. Contrasts may all share a common background yet remain poor contrasts by virtue of the *order* in which they unfold. Switch round the movements of a great sonata or a symphony and the new order will almost certainly be inferior to the old one. Again, other things being equal (key, tempo, time-signature, etc.), we cannot successfully mix the themes of one movement with those from another—even though they all come from the same work; the "new look" in most cases makes less sense. These simple facts demonstrate a principle, as I want to show.

Of all Beethoven's early piano sonatas, the *Pathétique* is, perhaps, the best known. Let us see what it can teach us about theme chronology. I propose to expose the work to a major piece of experimental surgery by taking one of its chief contrasting ideas and placing it in another part of the sonata. What will this demonstrate? First: that Beethoven's original theme distribution is superior. Second: that it *is* superior because the balance of structural tension in the re-distributed version is upset. Re-distribution, as we shall hear, blunts a masterpiece's impact. Consider the rondo finale's second subject.

EX. 71

Let us remove it from its original position; into the vacant site let us place part of the *first* movement's second subject, the passage that begins:

EX. 72

[Allegro di molto e con brio]

Will this theme take over the function of the other? In short, are
these two second subjects interchangeable? Listen to what happens
when we attempt so to regard them. Here is the Rondo with the
"foreign" contrast (see *):

EX. 73

RONDO: Allegro

[♩=♩ doppio movimento]

* (1st Movement: 2nd Subject)

Despite the semblance of continuity (I have transposed the "lead-
up" to the crucial join (*) into the minor mode so as to make the
new "second subject" as acceptable as possible) there remains something seriously wrong. The theme substitution does not work.
Why?

All composers know that you can convert contrasts into tension;
the bigger the one, the correspondingly greater the other. Nobody
understood this more than Beethoven—musical history's chief
tension-raiser. But if you increase contrasts above a certain point
the resulting tension becomes artistically unbearable, impossible to
assimilate; if you decrease them below a certain point, the resulting
tension may become all too easy to assimilate. Here lies a distinction
between the incomprehensible and the all-too-comprehensible,
between music which is meaningless and music whose meaning is

53

so obvious it bores us after a single hearing. In the *Pathétique* the first movement's second subject cannot assume the function of the rondo's second subject because it makes such a poor, low-tension contrast to the rondo's main theme, and it does so for the most concrete of musical reasons. It is not so much that these two themes are not like one another, do not belong to one another: they are, in fact, *too like* one another to stand in such close proximity (which must be why Beethoven placed them so far apart in the Sonata). Both themes are in the minor mode; both begin with identical motifs (see "X", Ex 73). To juxtapose these contrasts would have been a mistake in a work where structural tension is so high. It is instructive to compare the flaccid effect of Ex. 73 with Beethoven's original (Ex. 74).

A principle now suggests itself. A "right" thematic chronology is one which generates *maximum tension compatible with maximum comprehensibility*. Given the thousands of different ways in which the material of a masterpiece could be unfolded, a master chooses the one which maintains structural tension. He is guided, I submit, by a creative *principle of contrast distribution*.

Another work by Beethoven, his Fifth Symphony, corroborates this. The violent interplay of its contrasts, so characteristic of the work, makes it especially suitable for a demonstration of the

"chronology principle". Structural tension is maintained at a remarkably high level throughout, a fact we can readily demonstrate
by attempting to re-distribute Beethoven's contrasts. Almost any
other distribution results in a lowering of tension. In order to illu-
state this, I should like to move straight to the most vivid contrast
juncture in the Symphony's first movement, that of the abruptly
emerging second subject, in order to discover if there is a single
remaining theme in the entire Symphony which could *assume the
function*, maintain the tension, of that second subject. The passage
runs:

EX. 75

We shall quickly learn that there is no other theme in the Symphony capable of producing as violent a contrast *while remaining
comprehensible*. Indeed, so violent is this contrast that even Schoenberg found it interesting enough to analyse.[1] There is, perhaps, one
theme in the finale which could be brought forward as an experimental substitute, although the result, as can be heard, is such as to
prompt us hastily to return it to the point at which Beethoven himself introduces it.

[1] Essay: "Folkloristic Symphonies", *Style and Idea*, p. 200.

At *this* particular juncture, *that* particular contrast (which I have taken from the finale and transposed into E flat major) is unsatisfactory. A third-rate composer might have created it, but not Beethoven. It does not achieve anything like the tension of the original because, rhythmically, the new "second subject" is too *similar* to the first subject. Its incessant ♪♪♪|♩ ♪♪♪|♩ ♪♪♪|♩ bears too strong a resemblance to the rhythmic pattern of the opening ＞♫♫|♩ and monotony sets in. The theme is far more functional where Beethoven himself put it—as a foil to the finale's main idea, where it creates a vivid contrast.

The lesson is clear. Great contrasts develop out of one another, create a need for one another.

It might well be argued, especially by those with a "scientific" axe to grind, that my examples prove nothing, that the tension of a contrast is not something you can objectively measure, and that the so-called "chronology principle" is just another pile of rubble on the scrap-heap of personal opinion. There is only one reply to such an assertion. My examples do not try to "objectively measure" anything. They aim simply to enhance our *experience* of an intriguing aspect of musical structure. For the rest, if you cannot accept that the distribution of a masterwork's contrasts serves an artistic purpose, *is a symptom of its mastery*, then the onus is on you to bring forward an alternative theory explaining how great music can unfold in a random direction. The following might help to put the issue more clearly.

In 1822 the composer and publisher Diabelli invited fifty-one of the most prominent musicians then living in Austria and Germany to contribute a variation each on a Waltz-theme he himself had written. Everyone accepted—including Schubert, Moscheles, Czerny and the eleven-year-old Liszt—except Beethoven, who refused. Yet sometime afterwards Beethoven did, in fact, turn his attention to Diabelli's theme and his "contribution" flowered into the finest set of variations ever written. A comparison between these two sets is illuminating. "Diabelli's" set, by fifty different composers, is a curiosity of musical history. The chronology of the variations is governed not by any musical logic but by the alphabetical order of the composers' names! The musical results are ludicrous. Beethoven's set, on the other hand, unfolds a chronology which sounds absolutely right. I would stress that both sets are unified; they are, after all, based on a single theme. But the one remains a mediocrity while the other is a sublime masterpiece. One contributory factor to this distinction, I submit, is that the principle of contrast distribution operates in one, but not in the other. "Diabelli's" variations are thrown together casually. Beethoven's emerge *causally*.

Mahler's Symphony No. 6 in A minor contains a problem of interest in this context. The movements of the Symphony are: Allegro energico, ma non troppo: Andante moderato; Scherzo; and Sostenuto leading to Allegro energico. Mahler showed some indecision over the order of the middle movements. Prior to the publication of the Symphony, he had performed the work with the Scherzo second. But he later came to believe that the Scherzo would be better placed *third*; and that is how the Symphony was published. The Mahler society in Vienna, however, maintain that Mahler changed his mind yet again, reverting to the earlier chronology with the Scherzo second. The issue is by no means closed in Mahlerian circles, however.

In my view, the principle of contrast distribution clinches the matter. The published order has more to commend it musically than that advocated by the Mahler society.[1] *It creates a wider range of contrasts*—a range which, in a work of this length, is to be welcomed. It saves the Symphony from a long decline in structural tension which inevitably arises when the *Andante* is placed third and made to precede the finale's *Sostenuto*—no kind of contrast at all.

A similar structural problem arises in connection with Brahms's *Variations on a Theme by Paganini* (Op. 35). It illumines the principle of contrast distribution from the player's angle. Brahms published these variations in two books. Each book is self-contained. Quite frequently, however, both books are played in a single performance. Now, the most brilliant and extensive variation in both sets is the last in Book One. When both Books are played there is everything to be said for taking this last variation of Book One and placing it at the end of Book Two. You thereby remove the anti-climax inevitably created by playing this dynamic variation at the end of Book One and then moving on to the low-tension variations which begin Book Two. By introducing this slight change in the chronology of the variations the entire work builds up to an inexorable climax—to its advantage. Actually, this practice is becoming increasingly common among pianists. The principle of contrast distribution is, evidently, unconsciously pushing them towards a creative solution.

Schubert's C major String Quintet lends itself well to a demonstration of this principle. Having analysed the work in a previous section I do not question the unity of its themes. What I suggest is

EX. 77

[1] Deryck Cooke agrees with this observation. (Oral communication, December 1965.)

58

that the immense power of this structure derives, in part, from the way those themes are sited. Consider Ex. 77, the beginning of the Quintet. Hear what happens when we remove its second subject and transplant the *finale*'s second subject into the vacant site.

EX. 78

Again the question arises: Does the one theme take over the function of the other? There is not a single note in Ex. 78 that Schubert did not write. Indeed, we have here a *prima facie* passage of music. It is the *proximity* of the themes that is new. But when we consider the contrast potential offered by the material of the Quintet as a whole, we come to understand that this proximity is not ideal. It is flaccid. Schubert's original second subject is superior to the one transplanted above for the reason that its arrival generates great tension—a function of any respectable second subject. The totally unexpected side-slip into E flat major is one of the most compelling moments in all Schubert.

EX. 79

This is a dazzling contrast, much more interesting than my experimental replacement. A comparison of these two versions tells us a good deal about the function of second subjects. The whole point about a sonata structure is the integration of contrasts. The whole point about a second subject is to introduce them.

In short, I think that even though a masterwork's contrasting themes were to be completely re-shuffled (and the permutations are endless), the principle of contrast distribution would enable us eventually to divine their true chronology. The situation is somewhat analagous to that of a jig-saw puzzle. The bits are all there.

EX. 80

But there is only one assembly which is right. Similarly, there is one musical assembly which is right. This is the assembly which builds up maximum tension compatible with maximum comprehensibility. It is the one a master's creative unconscious instinctively propels him to unfold.

Before leaving this aspect of musical structure, let us consider a final example. It is more complex than the others; its theme interchange is more involved. I propose to take the entire exposition of Mozart's Piano Sonata in F major (K.332) and 're-compose' it. The exposition contains seven clearly defined, sharply contrasted themes. By re-distributing them, I aim once again to demonstrate the superiority of Mozart's original over all other permutations. I

[EX. 80 (cont.)]

ask only one favour of my readers: that Mozart's original version be considered side by side with mine.

My re-composed version *contains all Mozart's original material.* Mozart's exposition is 93 bars long; my exposition, too, is 93 bars long. The only (three) sounds which are not by Mozart occur at the three asterisks (bars 12, 67 and 92). These minute textural repairs were forced upon me in order to prevent a crisis in continuity. It is true that my thematic re-shuffle has led to certain themes being transposed from the tonic into the dominant, and vice versa, yet this has not radically interfered with the music's balance of keys. That is to say, in Mozart's version just over half the exposition unfolds in the dominant key, and this also happens in my version. Yet the difference between the two might almost be called spectacular. *It*

[EX. 80 (cont.)]

is due entirely to the new distribution of themes. The original version, a miniature masterpiece, unrolls, as we might expect, the strongest of thematic chronologies. The interplay of its contrasts is vivid and compelling. And the tension it projects is lost the moment Mozart's themes are re-distributed.

Superficially, my version works. (A "flow", of sorts, has at least been retained. If you do not already know Mozart's original, I do not think you will reject my version, although I hear no chance of your ever accepting it as the work of a genius. It could have been written by a minor eighteenth-century composer.) It cannot withstand close scrutiny, however. My first departure from Mozart occurs at bars 12–19. Here, I move straight into Mozart's "codetta" theme which, in the original, rounds off the exposition with a vigorous flourish. In its new position, however, it is doubly disastrous; that is, it comes from nowhere, it leads nowhere. The abrupt appearance of the left-hand broken-chord semiquavers sounds nonsensical. More important, the impact of the subsequent transition theme (bars 20–37), one of the most dynamic contrasts of the structure, is wrecked through its sounding too like the preceding contrast. Compare with Mozart (bars 21 f) where the effect is electrifying. The same kind of criticism holds true for my second subject in which I *reverse* the original appearance of Mozart's three main tunes (bars 38–53, 53–68 and 68–83 respectively). Bars 38 ff. are the work of an inferior composer. Tonally, they are far too shaky to *establish* the onset of a second subject; the new tonic chord (C major), desperately needed at the beginning of the tune (which is where this chord occurs in the original) appears too late to save the music from tonal ambiguity. It is true that the structure picks up at bars 53–68; indeed, the smooth manner in which this idea emerges out of the previous bars is by no means unconvincing. Yet this one moment of authentic-sounding Mozart is quickly dispelled. At bar 68 the *real* second subject turns up, so firmly rooted in C major the result sounds slightly comic. The one point at which a bit of tonal ambiguity might work is the very point where we are strenuously denied it. This is the price of the wholesale reversal of themes between bar 38 and bar 83. The new "codetta" theme (bars 83–93) has been transposed (in both senses) from its real position, where it was an extension of the first subject, to the end of the exposition. As codetta themes go, this one functions surprisingly well— until we recall the double bar and repeat sign. Once again, my version deprives Mozart of an effective contrast: my quiet ending leads back to his quiet beginning. Compare the effect that Mozart's original dynamic codetta theme (bars 12–19) has at this juncture. It works as a first-rate spring-board from which to dive in either of two directions: backwards, plunging into the first bar of the exposition; or forwards, plunging into the first bar of the development.

Every musician who is interested in musical form should experiment with examples of his own. A theme re-shuffle among the given ideas of a masterpiece is an artistic impossibility. The mere fact of attempting to carry one out brings home a cardinal principle of musical aesthetics.

★   ★   ★

In logic, there is a law known as the "law of parsimony". It defines a principle of argument: namely, that it is only necessary to postulate those premises that are required to reach a conclusion; no more, yet no less. The law of parsimony is, essentially, a law of economy. Good musical argument is likewise subject to a law of economy.[1] The reason may be summarised in two words: maximum comprehension. To introduce into musical communication either more material or less than is actually required to convey the meaning behind that communication leads to ambiguity and distortion.

Composers through the ages have been acutely aware of the need to express themselves with unremitting clarity.[2] Some succeed; many fail. Josef Suk once showed Brahms one of his youthful quartets. That Brahms was well aware of the function of economy is shown by his reply, characteristically pointed. "The essential thing is that every note should be in its place. I can't do that—nor can Dvorak—and you, of course, least of all."[3] Debussy expressed the same problem another way. "It is curious how two 'parasitic' measures can demolish the most solidly built edifice. This is just what has happened to me, and nothing can prevent it, neither long experience nor the most beautiful talent! It is instinct only—as old

---

[1] I use the term "economy" in its strictest sense. Economy not only involves the elimination of surplus: it also involves the preservation of essence. Too little is as uneconomical as too much.

[2] "Every move towards logic and coherence in composing is in fact a move towards communication."—Aaron Copland *Music and Imagination*, p. 47, Harvard, 1961.

[3] Related by Suk to Paul Wittgenstein. See *Brahms* by Peter Latham, Master Musicians Series.

as the world—which can save you!"[1] It was this same instinct, presumably, which led Richard Strauss to refine some of the denser textures in *Salomé* (when he conducted the opera at Dresden between the two World Wars) so as to make the vocal parts more audible.[2] Beethoven rarely succeeded in correctly articulating his ideas the first time. His Sketch Books put his creative process under a magnifying glass. They reveal an obsessive search for a true formulation. To "fix" the idea, to define it, to pin it down—that Beethoven knew this was of the essence came out strongly on one occasion when, after hearing the Funeral March from Paoer's opera *Achilles*, he observed: "I must compose that!"

Now the general law of economy which all these composers were hinting at, and which musicians of all times have had an unconscious awareness, divides into a group of subsidiary principles which I should like to define separately.

First: the principle of *identity between the idea and the utterance*. In a masterpiece, the "idea" and its "utterance" are one. To put this proposition another way: it is a function of creative mastery to clothe an idea with a certain number of notes; no more, yet no less. I derive this hypothesis from the simple observation that you distort a masterpiece the moment you add to it or subtract from it.

It may well be asked how I propose to demonstrate this proposition. The task is not easy. How do you distinguish between a thought and its utterance? How do you establish what a composer really *means* as opposed to what he actually *writes*?

I want to approach this thorny problem by easy stages.

Few composers formulate their ideas precisely the first time. They are constantly re-adjusting and re-defining until their "outer" notation matches their "inner" vision.[3] This habit of sketching offers us an ideal starting-point. Indeed, it brings into sharp focus the distinction I have already made between an "idea" and its "utterance". Beethoven's sketches are more fascinating than most—partly

[1] Letter to Jacques Durand, Paris, 21 March 1917.

[2] Leo Wurmser, Richard Strauss as an Opera Conductor, *Music and Letters*, Vol. 45, No. 1, January 1964.

[3] Composition is not the only field in which such "matching" occurs. Performers have the same problem too. The ideal towards which they strive is that of making their "outer" performance coincide in every respect with their "inner" conception of the music. Indeed, most of the self-criticism that goes on among performers arises from the distance their actual achievements fall short of their highest ideals.

because they reflect every stage of his creative process (often, even the sketches have sketches), and partly because the contrast between the initial, unpromising formulation and the final, inspired result is so spectacular. Every detail is exposed—like watching a film in slow motion.

The first time Beethoven articulated the main theme of the slow movement of his Fifth Symphony it emerged like this.

EX. 81

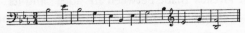

Only after it had been subjected to several re-workings was this elusive theme finally "fixed" by Beethoven.

EX. 82

Now it may be objected that, far from demonstrating a difference between "idea" and "utterance", these two examples show the utter futility of posing such a distinction in the first place. It could be maintained that there are two different ideas here, each with its own "utterance". There is a sense in which this is true. Equally, there is a sense in which it is false. Examine the intervening sketches, and you soon conclude that the final version *was contained in* the sketches from the start (like a perfect sculpture already contained in a rough slab of marble; a master would maintain it was merely a question of chipping away the unwanted pieces).

Here is an even clearer illustration, again from Beethoven's sketches. The Trio from the Scherzo of the *Eroica* Symphony was first notated by Beethoven in this way:

EX. 83

It was only later that he re-fashioned it into the version with which everybody is now familiar:

EX. 84

Allegro vivace

Again, when we study these two formulations with the other sketches, it is borne in on us that the finished version *was contained in* the rough drafts from the outset; that the "idea" and the "utterance" *converged* in the final version.

It is clear that sketches are of limited use to us in demonstrating the existence of the principle of identity between idea and utterance. They can furnish an illuminating starting-point; yet their great drawback is that the evidence they offer is *pre*-compositional. Sketches are not part of the work at all; they are means, not ends, and I only introduced them by way of furnishing an analogy. Let us push forward the argument a stage by returning to the finished composition itself.

There is a field of musical creation well suited to a demonstration of this principle. I refer to revisions. Most composers revise. They may return to "completed" works, often after an interval of many years, and re-compose them. Nothing could serve better to illustrate the presence of economic tendencies in creative genius. Revision is an acknowledgement by the composer himself that what he actually wrote is not what he actually meant. Revision is an act of self-criticism. It aims to re-define, and therefore enhance, a musical communication.[1]

When Liszt's *Transcendental Studies* (1839) were reviewed by Schumann he rightly described them as "studies of storm and dread for, at the most, ten or twelve players in the world". The interesting thing is that when Liszt revised them (1852) he simplified them——presumably to make them more accessible. Many of the original technical difficulties were smoothed out in the later version. More important in the present context, however, is the fact that Liszt chips away a great deal of the surplus material in which his ideas were originally embedded, giving them sharper definition. Here is

---

[1] The very word "revision" implies that a composer has a *re*-vision, a new vision of his work. True, what prompts him to revise may not always *seem* like a new vision. External conditions arise which sometimes force a composer to adapt his work. One thinks of Mozart re-composing operatic arias owing to last-minute cast changes. But this is not, strictly speaking, "revision" at all. It is the creation of genuine, musical *alternatives* which arise from a sense of expediency; and frequent as it is, it is not nearly so common as that caused by creative dissatisfaction. It is this last activity, revisions which are *artistically* determined, which discloses an unconscious drive towards economy.

a simple illustration. Liszt begins the first version of the Transcendental Study No. 8 ("Wilde Jagd") thus:

EX. 85

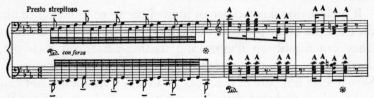

In the second version the texture has been simplified and, consequently, clarified.

EX. 86

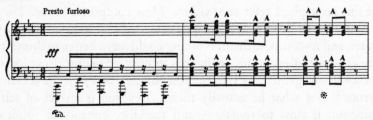

These examples, which should be compared in their entirety, emphasise the difference between the "idea" and the "utterance", between the immutable inspiration and the mutable notes which clothe it.

It could be held that these examples of revisions are open to precisely the same objection as my earlier examples of sketches. That is to say, the composer himself has accomplished the revision. What we have witnessed is an act of *self*-criticism—a very different thing from criticism! All this is true. Let me push the argument to its final stage.

Composers are not only self-critics. They are critics, too. When Beethoven said of Paoer's *Funeral March* "I must compose that", and when Brahms told Suk that "the essential thing is that every note should be in its place", they were defining a tool of criticism; they were comparing the *real* music, the music behind the notes, with the way in which it had been *wrongly* expressed. Such observations can sometimes lead to highly productive results. Composers will sometimes re-compose composers. This can be criticism on a grand, creative scale. So devastatingly effective can it be, the original composition can be totally replaced by the new version which succeeds where the other failed. History is full of examples.

Bach's "arrangement" for four harpsichords (in A minor) of Vivaldi's Concerto in B minor for four violins is more than an adaptation from one medium to another. It is an act of criticism *par excellence*. For Bach completely re-composes Vivaldi. So successfully does he accomplish the task that, as Alfred Einstein pointed out, Vivaldi's original composition has been obscured by Bach's adaptation. Bach lavished the whole of his genius on the work. He did not hesitate to enrich the texture where the original suggested this might be desirable. Compare these two examples:

EX. 87

Here we have a supreme example of a composer turned critic. Vivaldi created the idea. But it was left to Bach to show him how to

give it complete utterance. It is almost as though Vivaldi had
travelled ahead and temporarily composed the Concerto until Bach
could arrive on the scene and compose it for himself. One is reminded of Elgar's remark: "Works of art are not created; they are
there, waiting to be discovered."

In 1831 Liszt heard Paganini. The experience electrified him. He

EX. 89(a)

resolved to explore the full resources of the keyboard, just as Paganini had explored those of the violin. Seven years later, Liszt published his set of six *Paganini Studies*.[1] Five of them are transcriptions of pieces from Paganini's *Twenty-four Caprices* for unaccompanied violin. The remaining one, *La Campanella*, is based on the Rondo of Paganini's B minor Concerto. A comparison between the originals and Liszt's adaptations is revealing. Like Bach, Liszt does not hesitate to re-compose the originals. I do not mean he merely adapts to the new medium. He does this and much more. He adds new figurations, transforms the harmony and even adds extra bars. One of the best transcriptions in the set is the second, in E flat major (number 17 in the Paganini collection). See EXX. 89 (*a*) and (*b*).

EX. 89(*b*)

One is tempted to say of Liszt's version that it transformed the original not out of, but *into*, recognition. Posterity would scarcely remember this Paganini Caprice, if Liszt had not shown a creative interest in it. Hearing the two versions one after the other is like seeing a blurred image suddenly leap into sharp focus.

The method I have chosen to project this distinction between an "idea" and its "utterance" receives corroboration from an unexpected quarter. The very act of teaching composition is a tacit acknowledgement that you can not only diagnose a distinction be-

[1] Which, like the *Transcendental Studies*, were revised in 1852.

tween "idea" and "utterance" but that you can also remedy the situation. A good composition teacher does not merely re-compose his students' work. He helps them to search for its truer expression. It is his chief function to help his students to keep re-formulating the "utterance" until they have captured the "idea". Hindemith was aware of this principle when he talked about those "uncontested masterpieces [whose] particular kind of perfection, *the absolute coincidence of intention and realisation*, is almost superhuman".[1] [My italics.]

* * *

There are other directions, too, in which the creative tendency towards economy operates. One of the more important manifests itself as a principle of *Co-extension between form and content*. Debussy once told Satie that he should pay more attention to form. Satie responded by writing his *Trois Morceaux en forme de Poire* (Three pieces in the form of a Pear)! There was a right idea behind Debussy's advice, just as there was a right idea behind Satie's response. Debussy was regarding form as an *aim* of musical content; whereas Satie was trying to show that form is a *result* of musical content. Now many musicians have observed that the distinction between "form" and "content" is a false one. They rightly point out that you cannot have "form" without, at the same time, having "content", that the one is the organic result of the other, that it is misleading to talk about form as if it were an empty husk, a mould into which "content" is poured. "Form" and "content" are different aspects of the same thing. One of our leading composers recently put it quite neatly:

> Forms in music differ from those supplied by H.M. Inspector of Taxes; they are not there to be filled in.[2]

Ernest Newman summed up the problem this way:

> The form of a musical work is good when the work is neither too short nor too long for its subject, and when each bar of the music follows logically on the bar before it and leads logically into the bar that comes after it.[3]

There is, then, no such thing as Form with a capital F; there are only

[1] Hindemith, *A Composer's World*, 1952, p. 73.
[2] Alan Rawsthorne, "Chopin's Ballades and Scherzos", *ibid.*
[3] *Sunday Times*, 30 December 1922.

73

individual forms. Yet, in their attempts to escape the dead hand of academicism, where forms are merely "there to be filled in", these musicians (and I am with them all the way; indeed, I push their case further than they do) overlook a basic aesthetic problem. All music has form; but not all music has good form. If form and content are one, how do we *know*, *pace* Newman, that the form of a piece of music is "too short"? How do we *know* that it is "too long"?

The process is one of the most mysterious in all music criticism; yet it works. I contend that when we understand music really well, when it has become a part of us, we also intuitively come to know the *potential* of its material. It is the non-fulfilment of this potential that enables us to diagnose a "split" between content and form, between the distance the music has already covered and the distance it might yet cover, between what the music actually is and what it could still become. Why is a masterpiece as long as it is? Text-books on form remain silent. Yet it is of paramount interest to know why music ends when it does. The one sure thing about a masterpiece is that it completes its allotted span with the punctuality of a planet completing its orbit. Music has a certain propensity to unfold a certain distance. If it stops before it has done so, it is incomplete. If it goes on after it has done so, it is over-complete; there is no room in great music for the pleonasm.[1]

Of course, the stop-watch length of music has nothing to do with this principle. Chopin's Prelude in C sharp minor is very tiny by comparison with Beethoven's *Eroica* Symphony. The one unfolds about thirty seconds' music; the other about fifty minutes'. Yet both works are exactly the right length for their material whose potential is fully realised. The Chopin prelude is of such brevity that I can quote it in full.

[1] An interesting side-issue is raised by the question: Why do symphonies usually have four movements, while concertos usually only have three?
I am aware that there is an historical answer, that tradition and convention play a role. But unless they are aesthetically workable, there are no conventions to discuss: they do not survive long enough. It is not sufficient to say that symphonies have four movements and concertos have three because that is the number of movements history says they should have. The reason is purely musical. Concertos can generate just as wide a range of contrasts in three movements as symphonies can in four. So a fourth would be redundant. Other things being equal, ideas unfolded in terms of the concerto's ripieno-concertino duality, in which the material flits back and forth between opposing groups of players, will achieve their full contrast potential in fewer movements than those which are not.

74

I invite the reader to subtract from or add to this miniature master-piece just a single bar. The resulting distortion will demonstrate that the "form" and the "content" are indivisible.

*   *   *

There functions in all great music a *principle of audibility*. To get across, to make a *total* aural impact; that is an objective towards which all notes travel. Not all of them arrive.

On the most primitive level, anything in a musical structure which is strictly inaudible is strictly unnecessary: if you cut it out, you cannot hear the difference, anyhow. But this kind of inaudibility is not all that fruitful to study. I know of no great master who is guilty of such gross miscalculations (although I can think of several lesser masters who are).[1] All the examples of inaudibility I shall discuss

[1] An objective test, which, admittedly, calls for musicianship of a high order, is to re-construct from the sounds alone the score in question. To capture and notate music through the ears alone is a symptom, at the very least, that it is coming across.

actually work against the musical argument which, in consequence, is heard to suffer. All are drawn from major masterpieces; a minor blemish on a major masterpiece is, by virtue of its context, under a spotlight to begin with. Some of them are trivial; it is possible to "save" them by care in performance. Others are more serious. At least one approaches a major aural disaster.[1]

The recapitulation in the first movement of Beethoven's Eighth Symphony has often been criticised on the grounds of its inaudibility. As Tovey observed: "It is not easy to make out the tune with all the noontide glare beating down over it".[2]

EX. 91

In many respects the orchestration, which is top heavy, works against the theme in the bass. For once, Beethoven's almost infallible sense of orchestration seems to have let him down. The potential inaudibility of this passage gives a clear mandate to the conductor who can, if he is aware of the problem, balance the orchestra in such a way that the bass theme can be heard.

A rather similar, and equally familiar, case of potential inaudibility which can be rectified in performance, occurs in the finale of Tchaikovsky's Fourth Symphony. The explosive *fff* passage (Ex. 92) which ends with a thunderclap on the bass drum and cymbals (bar 2) swamps the delicate, incoming texture (bar 3) in a mighty tidal-wave of sound. The new B flat minor theme on soft woodwind, is barely heard beneath the massive reverberation of the previous bar which rolls round the hall for several seconds. Most conductors are aware of the trap and take evasive action. Although Tchaikovsky has not marked the score in this way, it is now almost mandatory to pause before the new theme at bar 3 until the rever-

[1] The Grieg Piano Concerto. See Ex 97.
[2] *Essays in Musical Analysis*, Vol. I, p. 64.

beration has disappeared. It is, in fact, the only way of rendering the immediately subsequent texture audible.

EX. 92

In the second movement of Brahms's Symphony No. 1 in C minor, the onset of the recapitulation is in perennial danger of being obscured. At the point where the first theme of the movement returns, Brahms gives it to *pianissimo* woodwind; the strings, which originally presented the theme, now have a new line doubled at the octave and the sixteenth.

EX. 93

The woodwind theme is usually very difficult to hear, for most conductors (aided and abetted by Brahms) swamp it in a romantic surge of sound from the strings. This is a disaster from the structural point of view, for this theme is the beginning of the recapitulation. No matter what subsequent thematic repetition we hear, the vital impact of initial return is lost.

An example of "built-in" inaudibility, well known among chamber music players, is the third variation of the slow movement of Beethoven's C minor Piano Trio, Op. 1.

77

The pizzicato strings cannot make themselves heard against the brilliant piano part—the more brilliantly it is played, the less audible they become.

In 1937 Schoenberg completed an orchestration of Brahms's Piano Quartet in G minor, Op. 25. His reasons are revealing. They are not the usual ones. That is to say, he was not interested simply in transferring the music from one medium to another for the sake of the "colour effects"—as, for example, Ravel was when orchestrating Mussorgsky's *Pictures at an Exhibition*. Schoenberg's aims were far more functional. As a young man, he had played the Brahms Piano Quartet on many occasions both as a violist and as a cellist. Time and again, he was struck by its potential inaudibility. The piano tends to swamp the strings. Schoenberg expressed it thus:[1] "It is always very badly played, because, the better the pianist,

[1] In a letter to Alfred Frankenstein of the *San Francisco Chronicle*, dated 1939 *Letters*, (ed. Erwin Stein), London, 1964.

the louder he plays and you hear nothing from the strings. I wanted once to hear everything, and this I achieved." The orchestration is, in fact, an exercise in musical audibility—one master helping another to get across —and has few parallels in music's history.

Mahler's re-orchestrations of Schumann's symphonies were likewise accomplished in the interests of audibility. There is an excellent example of Mahler "putting across" Schumann in the first movement of the *Rhenish* Symphony. At one point, Schumann states his first subject in canon. He divides the canon between upper strings (doubled by horns) and woodwind. Orchestrated like this, the leading voice is much more powerful than the trailing voice; indeed, it obscures it.[1]

[1] Deryck Cooke drew my attention to this passage. See also "Mahler's Re-scoring of the Schumann Symphonies", Mosco Carner, *Music Review*, Vol. II, No. 2.

Mahler's version puts the passage into better aural perspective. By transferring the horns to the trailing voice (and making other subtle adjustments, notably the suppression of Schumann's wayward timpani parts c.f.) he renders the canon highly audible. Schumann enthusiasts, I know, have strongly objected to Mahler's alterations. There are two simple replies. First: Mahler himself was a Schumann enthusiast. Second: Schumann wrote a canon. He wanted it to be heard.

One of the most striking cases of inaudibility occurs towards the end of Grieg's A minor Piano Concerto, where the theme of the finale's central episode returns in full orchestral splendour, and where it obliterates the solo pianist totally and absolutely.

In the concert hall[1] it is an extraordinary effect to see the soloist racing up and down the keyboard, *fortissimo*, apparently without producing any sound. The observation is beyond all question, and I invite anyone to check it for himself the next time he sees the Concerto played on the stage. The conclusion you draw, of course, will depend largely on whether you think that Grieg *meant* it to be

[1] Gramophone records are different. The balance between orchestra and piano can be artificially controlled so that, paradoxically, the notes come across despite Grieg, rather than because of him.

heard. I personally think that he did, and I consider it a serious miscalculation in a work which is otherwise supremely well composed.

*   *   *

At the beginning of my book I described music's creative principles as *a priori* because, as I put it, they are there before the beginning: a masterpiece is inconceivable without them; a mediocrity is inconceivable with them. In the interests of clarity I want to summarise the philosophical position into which such a view leads us.

Buridan, a logical philosopher of the 14th century,[1] was reputed to own a remarkable ass. Placed between two bundles of hay, the animal is said to have correctly deduced that both were equally succulent. It then starved to death because it could discover no rational reason for proceeding in one direction rather than the other. This astonishing beast was well on the way to becoming a bad music critic. Indeed, asked to decide between two works, many a critic might follow its example; that is to say, having exhausted his intellect weighing one possibility against another, he might be faced with a logical obligation to starve himself into silence. So much the worse for the intellect. So much the worse, too, for musical criticism. I have never understood the somewhat exalted position to which Buridan's ass has been raised by some philosophers. It has always seemed to me fully deserving of its fate. But perhaps this is because my own philosophical position is different. Essentially, that position is a Pragmatic one. Had Buridan's ass been a Pragmatist, it would have consumed both bundles of hay and "rationalised" the event later. Likewise criticism. We "consume" music, then we "rationalise" the experience. It is simply not true that critics wait until they have set a masterpiece against a critical yardstick before they know that it *is* a masterpiece. Criticism does not work like that. Music's value is there, *a priori*; it comes across intuitively as part of the musical communication. You know, you criticise (=rationalise); the converse is unthinkable.

Pragmatism must have the gravest consequences for the so-called "scientific" school of musical criticism. In fact, the crucial problem of that school was never solved. It was doomed from the start. There is no scientifically valid method of proving that your "objective" criteria are truly objective. The dilemma is this: if, on the one hand, you deduce "criteria" from your musical experience, they are not objective; if, on the other, you do not, they are irrelevant. By contrast, my theory takes it as a pragmatically established fact that (say) Mozart's *Jupiter* Symphony is a masterpiece. Criticism did not establish that fact; Mozart did. The function of criticism, as I see it, is to attempt to explain, *post factum*, why Mozart was successful.

[1] 1300–50.

From time to time, I have observed that the creative process, like the critical, is an intuitive activity. Music cannot communicate, let alone survive, unless it expresses a high degree of unconscious content. The unconscious is the womb of musical creation; all masterpieces are born there.

Such categorical assertions are likely to sound provocative. They impute to the musical unconscious almost uncanny powers of creative organisation. Yet there is a great deal of evidence, from composers themselves, suggesting unconscious sources for their ideas. Many of them have self-confessedly picked their way through the complexities of a composition as if in a sleepwalking trance. Indeed, there are a great many so-called "intellectual" achievements in music which were arrived at with no more effort than it requires to produce a dream. My comparison is nearer the mark than may be supposed. Composers who dream music are not at all uncommon.

Let me give some instances of the organising powers of the musical unconscious; they will help to prepare the ground for the theory of unconscious communication between composers and listeners which I want to put forward in Part Three.

On one occasion Tartini gave an account of how he came to compose his *Devil's Trill* sonata to the great astronomer Lalande:

> One night I dreamt that I made a bargain with the Devil for my soul. Everything went at my command; my new servant anticipated every one of my wishes. Then I conceived the idea of handing him my violin, to see what he could do with it. Great was my astonishment when I heard him play a sonata of such exquisite beauty as surpassed the boldest flight of my imagination. I awoke, and seizing my violin, I tried to reproduce the sound I had heard, but in vain. The sonata I then composed, although the best I ever wrote, was far below the one I heard in my dream.

Even Schoenberg and Stravinsky, two of the most "cerebral" composers of the age, are self-confessed sleepwalkers. Schoenberg tells us that after he had completed his First Chamber Symphony (1906) he became worried by the apparent lack of connection between two of its themes, although this thought had not bothered him while he was actually composing the work. After a great deal of mental torture, he decided to stand by his initial inspiration. Twenty years later, he suddenly became aware of the true connection. The themes were linked by a complex serial procedure—and this, eighteen years before Schoenberg himself officially discovered serialism.[1] As for Stravinsky, not only is he known to compose music in his dreams but he has confessed to using some of his dream music in his actual compositions. While working on *L'Histoire du Soldat* Stravinsky had a dream in which a young gipsy girl was sitting on the edge of the road playing a violin. She kept repeating the same motif

EX. 98

which, Stravinsky tells us, he found so attractive that when he woke up he included it in the music of the *Petit Concert*.[2]

The latest scientific evidence suggests that the duration of a dream is very short—no more than a few seconds; yet composers have been known to dream entire compositions, sometimes long and complex. "Dream music", in fact, proves the *simultaneity* of the creative act. The dream is the window of the unconscious, and the unconscious refuses to recognise time.[3] The lightning flashes of inspiration which composers of all generations have experienced merely illumine something which is already there and which simply needs to be formulated. "Shortness" and "longness" are terms which are rendered meaningless in the context of the timeless unconscious. Mozart summed it up when he once talked about perceiving his music all at once "like a beautiful statue".

Mahler has related an astonishing story about the composition of his Eighth Symphony (The *Symphony of a Thousand*). He said that while setting the *Veni Creator* he suddenly felt compelled to insert an extensive orchestral passage between two stanzas without knowing why. About the same time, he became suspicious of the Latin text he was using and sent it to his friend Fritz Löhn with an urgent

[1] *Style and Idea*, p. 113, London, 1951.
[2] *Conversations with Igor Stravinsky*, Igor Stravinsky and Robert Craft, p. 17, London, 1959.
[3] Psycho-analysts have often observed that music forms an important link in the chain of their patients' free associations. (See *The Haunting Melody: Psycho-Analytic Experiences in Life and Music* by Theodor Reik, New York, 1963.)

request that he translate it (superficially, an unnecessary act; although Mahler did not read Latin, he must have understood the *Veni* otherwise he would hardly have embarked on its composition in the first place). Löhn saw at once that Mahler's text was incomplete, and when he had returned the complete text in translation Mahler discovered that the missing words *exactly fitted the orchestral passage that he had meanwhile composed.* This event might appear inexplicable were it not for the fact that years earlier Mahler had read the *Veni Creator* in Goethe's translation and had subsequently "forgotten" it. Yet it is clear that he had retained a vivid, unconscious memory of it from the fact that his *musical* unconscious had insisted on providing the music for the "missing" text.[1] Perhaps only those who themselves have set words to music can fully grasp the astonishing feat of unconscious organisation involved here.

Sir William Walton has reported that the 12-note row comprising the *Passacaglia* theme in the finale of his Second Symphony occurred to him "quite fortuitously".[2]

EX. 99

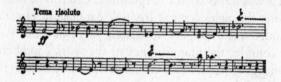

Walton's observation is an interesting example of the way in which the musical unconscious can prompt thematic material to unfold in a "strictly organised" manner.

The musical unconscious may often work so secretly that it is only when a composer sits down "to compose" that he mysteriously discovers that he has nothing whatever to do except to notate the ideas as they flood into his conscious mind. When Schubert was seventeen he wrote a string quartet in B flat major. The first movement, comprising 264 bars, was composed in four and a half hours.[3] Even an expert copyist could hardly match this feat! Schubert also composed *Erlkönig* in a single, inspired flash. His friend, Joseph von Spaun, has related how he and Mayerhofer went to visit Schubert one

---

[1] See Theodor Reik, *op. cit.*
[2] Murray Schafer, *British Composers in Interview*, p. 79, London, 1963.
[3] See Deutsch catalogue No. 112.

afternoon and found him excitedly pacing his room reciting Goethe's verses from a book in his hand. "Suddenly Schubert sat down and, in the shortest time one can imagine, the magnificent ballad was on paper. Since Schubert had no piano, we ran to the convent close by, and it was there that the *Erlkönig* was sung the very same evening."[1] Of a similar kind is Schoenberg's achievement in the composition of *Erwartung*—a highly complex score of 426 bars which he completed within the astonishing time of twenty days.[2] Better known are the stories concerning the composition of Mozart's *Don Giovanni* overture and Berlioz's *Marche au Supplice* from the Fantastic Symphony. Both movements were written in a single night. Examples could be multiplied indefinitely of works which seemed to spring "fully armed" from the minds of their composers. Handel composed *Messiah* within the period 22 August to 12 September 1741. The first part consists of one hundred pages of manuscript and finishes with the date 28 August; that is to say, Handel composed it in six days. The second part, which is longer than the first, bears the final date 6 September. The final part comprises fifty-one pages of manuscript and it was finished on 12 September. In terms of sheer physical labour alone this achievement has few parallels in history; at one stage, Handel was averaging seventeen pages of score a day. And when we consider the magnificence of the work's total conception and its unflagging inspiration, we must regard *Messiah* as one of the miracles of artistic creation.

On the manuscript of his Overture in F major for piano duet Schubert scribbled the following remark: "In November (1819) in the room of Mr. Joseph Huettenbrenner in the Civic Hospital— written in three hours and skipped lunch because of it." The Overture is 258 bars long! Of course, unconscious creation is by no means synonymous with speed. Rather is it synonymous with discovery— a discovery of something which already exists on an unconscious level.[3] Beethoven, for example, often had to conquer his music

[1] Deutsch, *Schubert Brevier*, Berlin, 1905.

[2] See *The Works of Arnold Schoenberg*. A catalogue of his compositions by Josef Rufer, p. 34, London, 1962.

[3] It is symptomatic of the intuitive way in which Chopin composed that even while he was working on his *Polonaise-Fantaisie* he could not identify its true character. In a letter to his family (December 1845) he referred to a new work "something I don't know how to name" which flowered of its own volition into one of his most original forms, with Chopin, apparently, passively observing its development. In this connection I am reminded of a remark of Stravinsky's who,

bar by bar; but he always knew what his ultimate goal was. And even Haydn became desperate over the creation of *The Creation*— a truly Freudian situation—which would not seem to come out right. Composers may have to revise many times before they succeed in fully projecting their inner vision.

The musical unconscious not only starts the creative process: it can stop it as well. There are plenty of cases of composers who were unable to bring major works to completion. Schoenberg, for example, never finished his Oratorio *Jacob's Ladder* (1917–22) although he wanted to, and he made several attempts to do so during the remaining thirty years of his life. Commentators sometimes try to explain this by pointing to "external" causes. It is true that Schoenberg's career was disrupted twice by military service during the First World War; it is also true that his request for a Guggenheim award (1945) to help him buy the time necessary to complete the work was turned down. Yet Schoenberg wrote many of his most important works while being unable to finish *Jacob's Ladder*. This fact needs explaining. At bottom, we can detect what psychologists would call a "will to fail". For some mysterious reason, known only to his creative unconscious, Schoenberg, it seems, did not want to finish the work.

The trance-like condition which can accompany an act of musical creation was described on one occasion by Wagner while discussing the initial inspiration of the orchestral prelude to *Rhinegold*. After entering a "cataleptic state" he suddenly felt, he says, as if he were sinking into a mighty flood:

> The rush and roar soon took musical shape within my brain as the chord of E flat major surged incessantly in broken chords: these declared themselves as melodic figurations of increasing motion, yet the pure triad of E flat major never changed, but seemed by its steady persistence to impart infinite significance to the element in which I was sinking. I awoke from my half-sleep in terror, feeling as though the waves were now rushing high above my head. I at once recognised that the orchestral prelude

when asked about *Le Sacre* emphasised his *passive* role in its creation. "I heard and I wrote what I heard. I am the vessel through which *Le Sacre* passed."
Expositions and Developments, London, 1959.

to the *Rhinegold* which for a long time I must have carried about within me, yet had never been able to fix definitely, had at last come to being within me.[1]

I think it would be a mistake to dismiss this kind of testimony—highly coloured though it is.[2] It is of the utmost interest to the student of modern psychology. And Wagner only confirms what many other composers have also experienced. Even Brahms testifies to the inspired trance.

Straightway the ideas flow in upon me, directly from God and not only do I see distinct themes in my mind's eye, but they are clothed in the right forms, harmonies and orchestration. Measure by measure, the finished composition is revealed to me when I am in those rare, inspired moods, as they were to Tartini when he composed his greatest work—the *Devil's Trill* Sonata. I have to be in a semi-trance condition to get such results.[3]

It would be fascinating to know which of his works Brahms was talking about. Critics still tend to regard his music as "contrived".

Aaron Copland has put on record some surprisingly similar observations about musical inspiration.

The inspired moment may sometimes be described as a kind of hallucinatory state of mind: one half of the personality emotes and dictates while the other half listens and notates. The half that listens had better look the other way, had better simulate a half attention only, for the half that dictates is easily disgruntled and avenges itself for too close inspection by fading entirely away.[4]

Such a wealth of testimony about the creative process I find compelling. It points towards my earlier arguments. A master unconsciously harnesses musical principles in the service of his genius. They are the "hidden persuaders" which prompt us to recognise him.

[1] Quoted from Newman's *Life of Wagner*, Vol. II, p. 361.
[2] To judge from his frequent remarks on the subject, Wagner had an unusually keen insight into the creative process. In *Meistersinger*, it will be recalled, even the inspiration for the "Prize Song" comes to Walter in a dream!
[3] Quoted from *Talks with the Great Composers*, by Arthur M. Abell.
[4] Aaron Copland, *Music and Imagination*, p. 43, Harvard, 1961.

Part Three

A Theory of Unconscious Assimilation

I HAVE called those creative principles which shape a masterpiece its "hidden persuaders". Why do they sometimes fail? Why is a masterpiece recognised by some people and not by others?

This is one of the great problems of musical criticism. It would seem to destroy our theory at its roots. For it is all very well to maintain, for the sake of an hypothesis, that musical communication is potentially universal;[1] but to pretend that this notion is borne out in reality is to show crass indifference to the facts. Indeed, the kaleidoscopic variety of response that music invariably provokes among listeners is a notorious quicksands; more than one "scientific" theory of musical criticism has marched straight into it and has, mercifully, been swallowed whole. It may appear, then, that I am courting disaster in attempting to rest my own theory on those same treacherous foundations. As we shall see, however, no foundation could be safer—providing we first come to understand it. The listener's response is the most concrete piece of evidence we have to rely on. It is *there*. Let us begin by acknowledging that when music brings home a crop of contradictory reactions it is a *symptom of people, not music*. It is to psychology that we must turn for some answers.

Everybody has experienced those mysterious moments of revelation when, in a sudden shaft of illumination, "understanding" floods in. One moment we do not comprehend; the next, we do. It is as if we had arrived via an unconscious "leap in the dark". This "leap in the dark" cannot be invoked; it can only be experienced. It is as if certain works and certain listeners *attracted* one another,

[1] See p. 9.

while certain other works and listeners *repelled* one another. Can this be fortuitous? I do not believe that it can. I believe that there is a highly selective principle at work, a principle which *pre-determines* our basic responses towards music. It is a *principle of unconscious identification*. Where there is no unconscious identification, there is no musical understanding either. What purpose could such a principle possibly serve? The mechanism of unconscious identification is clearly something we must examine in greater detail.

The concept was first introduced by Freud in his epoch-making book *The Interpretation of Dreams* and it rapidly developed into one of the major tools of psycho-analysis. To my knowledge, it has only once before been used as a tool of musical criticism.[1] The term "unconscious identification" describes an important psychological mechanism. In its strictest sense, it stands for the tendency all developing personalities have to incorporate someone else's ego-traits into their own. The growing personality unconsciously swallows, digests, assimilates those character-traits it admires so that it, too, may possess and exhibit them in a like degree. There is no personality development without identification. This, I submit, applies equally to the development of *artistic* personality. History is full of composers who successfully developed by swallowing the artistic character-traits of other composers and digesting them into a satisfactory synthesis. On the other hand, there are also other composers, weaker personalities to be sure, who identify so compulsively with others, incorporating so much of their musical ego from outside, they lose their real identity and become a mere extension of their more powerful models.[2] For the ordinary musical listener, the process is complete and absolute. He is, as it were, a dumb composer who makes music by proxy. It is one of his symptoms of identification that, whenever he hears the work in question, it is as if he himself were creating it.[3] This is the music he would compose if he

[1] By Hans Keller. See *Stravinsky in Rehearsal* by Cosman and Keller, London 1962.

[2] It is not entirely irrelevant to point out that whenever identification has taken place "below the surface", the superficially descriptive historian starts talking about "schools", "trends", "movements", etc., as if a composer joined a school out of a sense of history! There are no genuine schools that are not held together by unconscious fetters. A composer "joins" because he is psychologically dependent upon the artistic ego-ideal of its leader.

[3] An observation which, I see, I arrived at independently of the Hungarian psychologist, G. Révész:

"It is also characteristic of the musical person to sink himself into the mood of

possessed the creative faculty. Of course, only when the "listener" happened at the same time to be a composer, should we ever have an opportunity of observing this tendency working itself out. But this does happen; occasionally, composers make music by proxy, too. One of the most remarkable cases of this kind, a symptom of deep-rooted identification, was Glazunov's reconstruction of the overture to Borodin's *Prince Igor*. Borodin, who played the piece several times to Glazunov, died without ever having put it down on paper. When Glazunov and Rimsky-Korsakov took over the task of completing the opera, Glazunov was able to write out the overture from memory. I am not illustrating Glazunov's prodigious memory-machine. The interesting question in these cases is not that memory-machines work: it is that they work most perfectly when their possessor is emotionally committed. They have been known to break down in the presence of an emotional blockage, or, as I should prefer to put it, in the absence of unconscious identification.

What, then, is the compulsive force behind identification? Why are we prompted to identify with some works and not with others? I confess that these are not easy questions to answer. Again, psychology provides a vital clue.

Art is an expression of libido—the primal, psychic force which resides within the repressed unconscious. To psycho-analysts, this notion is self-evident. To artists, however, it is often repugnant. For how can libido, which generates the sexual life of man, build a Parthenon, paint a Mona Lisa, compose an *Eroica*? The chief characteristic of libido is its mobility. Repress it, and it will seek an outlet elsewhere: it will replace its sexual aims with non-sexual ones—will *sublimate* them.[1] Hereafter, it becomes a building-force with wide-ranging potential. But no matter how remotely it builds, it remains in close touch with the erotic life of man, expresses it.[2]

---

the music and achieve a relation to it that has an effect on his whole spiritual being. He experiences the art-work so inwardly and so profoundly *that he feels as though he were creating it.*" [My italics.]

Introduction to the Psychology of Music, p. 134, London, 1953.

[1] Sublimation is an essential mechanism in growing up. Where libido remains fixated to its earlier modes of expression, to that extent those expressions remain infantile.

[2] One of the classical doctrines of psycho-analysis is that civilisation itself is created through repressed sexuality. Without repression, man would remain

During the years 1915–17 Freud delivered a series of lectures at the University of Vienna on psycho-analysis. One of them ended with a highly influential passage from which was developed the official psycho-analytical view about the origins of the artistic impulse.

Before you leave today I should like to direct your attention to a side of phantasy-life of very general interest. There is, in fact, a path from phantasy back again to reality, and that is—art. The artist has an introverted disposition and has not far to go to become neurotic. He is one who is urged on by instinctive needs which are too clamorous; . . . like any other with an unsatisfied longing, he turns away from reality and transfers all his interest, and all his Libido, too, on to the creation of his wishes in the life of phantasy, from which the way might readily lead to neurosis. There must be many factors in combination to prevent this becoming the whole outcome of his development; it is well known how often artists in particular suffer from partial inhibition of their capacities through neurosis. Probably their constitution is endowed with a powerful capacity for sublimation and with a certain flexibility in the repressions determining the conflict. But the way back to reality is found by the artist thus: He is not the only one who has a life of phantasy; the intermediate world of phantasy is sanctioned by general human consent, and every hungry soul looks to it for comfort and consolation. But to those who are not artists the gratification that can be drawn from the springs of phantasy is very limited; their inexorable repressions prevent the enjoyment of all but the meagre day-dreams which can become conscious. A true artist has more at his disposal. First of all he understands how to elaborate his day-dreams, so that they lose that personal note which grates upon strange ears and become enjoyable to others; he knows, too, how to modify them sufficiently *so that their origin in prohibited sources is not easily detected.* [My italics.] Further, he possesses the mysterious ability to mould his particular material until it expresses the ideas of his phantasy

---

(mentally, at any rate) an infant. Because most of his early, infantile impulses are prohibited, the individual represses them and learns instead to express much of instinctual life through a whole new range of sublimated activities. One of these activities is undoubtedly art.

faithfully; and then he knows how to attach to this reflection of his phantasy-life so strong a stream of pleasure that, for a time at least, the repressions are outbalanced and dispelled by it. When he can do all this, he opens out to others the way back to the comfort and consolation of their own unconscious sources of pleasure. . . .[1]

It is, then, with the composer's repressed unconscious that the listener compulsively identifies. He recognises something of his own personality in the work in question—even though it lies in those dark, fluid regions deep below the surface. The inspired idea, the inspired masterpiece, is one which is unconsciously invested, at the deepest creative level, with large quantities of libido; consequently, it has the power to release libido in all who identify with it. As I expressed it elsewhere, the successful composer–listener relationship is a love-affair, a blissful communion of unconscious minds.[2]

The key factor in our theory is *pre-determination*. If we take a panoramic view of the situation, all we see initially is a shifting, kaleidoscopic variety of composer–listener relationships. Listeners moving towards and away from composers; composers moving towards and away from listeners; works drifting aimlessly across the face of history, sometimes making contact, sometimes not. Small wonder, then, that a superficial glance at the problems of musical communication tends to bewilder us by the complexity and multiplicity of its phenomena. In fact, this mass of conflicting evidence only makes sense when we postulate the presence of an *unconscious principle of attraction and repulsion*. Far from being an haphazard affair, the composer–listener relationship is as strictly pre-determined by that principle as are the various trajectories of the fragments of an explosion by the laws of physics. Composers and listeners are, I

---

[1] *Introductory Lectures on Psycho-Analysis*, Freud, p. 314, London, 1952.
[2] I think this explains why great composers make such notoriously bad critics. So completely do they identify with their own sound-world, they are incapable of properly identifying with the sound-world of others. Tchaikovsky disliked Brahms. Brahms disliked Wagner. In our own time, Stravinsky disliked Schoenberg. Such emotional "demarcation disputes" are highly revealing unconscious symptoms and they serve a vital function. They protect the composer's artistic ego against those of "rival" composers. In fact, an inability to identify is a symptom that a composer has reached full maturity. He no longer has any artistic need to incorporate another's personality traits into his own and what might formerly have been "liking" turns, by way of self-protection, into "disliking".

submit, unconsciously *destined* to understand one another, just as they are unconsciously destined to misunderstand one another. Where you do not identify with a composer, you both have a problem. His is you; yours is him.

We are now in a position to consider one of the great paradoxes of musical criticism: the confrontation of two critics whose views about the same work are diametrically opposed. Musicians who are sceptical about a rational approach to musical criticism tend vigorously to polish the horns of this particular dilemma in the mistaken belief that the more brightly they shine the more impossible the dilemma will be to resolve. Let us accept their challenge. Let us pose their argument as forcefully as they might pose it themselves. And then, in the light of what we have learned about unconscious identification, let us demolish it.

Critic A loves a work; he has known it for years and has become deeply involved in it; he considers it a masterpiece. Critic B dislikes this same work; he, too, has known it for years but, for some mysterious reason, he cannot become involved in it at all; he considers it a mediocrity. Whom do we believe? They cannot both be right.[1] Let us assume that we ourselves have never heard the work; there is, therefore, no danger of our unconsciously "taking sides". Now the dilemma is resolved as soon as we realise that these critics lie within different, pre-selected fields of communication. Indeed, only by assuming that the work in question *is* a communication does the "confrontation" make sense. The great difference between critic A and critic B is that A is behaving like a man who has received a communication, while B is behaving like a man who has not. A's reaction is positive; it must stand for something which is *there*, for something he has experienced. B's reaction is negative; to be sure, it could stand for something which is *not* there, for something he has *not* experienced, were it not for the presence of A's positive reaction *which gives it the lie*.[2] B may protest as much as he likes that his negative testimony is just as valid as A's positive testimony. It is not. B is rather in the position of Alice who was standing with the White King waiting for his messengers.

[1] I do not accept that a critic can honestly dislike a work while honestly declaring at the same time that it is a masterpiece. This is a psychological impossibility. Under these conditions, he has absolutely no grounds for making such an assertion.

[2] "A bell does not ring by accident"—Plautus.

"I see nobody on the road," said Alice.

"I only wish I had such eyes," the King remarked in a fretful tone. "To be able to see Nobody, and at that distance too."

B's ears are no better than Alice's eyes. He can hear Nothing no clearer than she can see Nobody.

Let me give a further analogy. Two radio receivers are switched on. One of them receives a transmission; the other remains "dead". We do not conclude that the "dead" receiver indicates that nothing is being transmitted. On the contrary, we know that the "live" receiver proves that something *is* being transmitted. Consequently, we are led to assume that the "dead" receiver is incapable of functioning on that particular wavelength. A masterpiece, too, pours out a flood of information, irrespective of the number of "receivers" tuned in to it. It operates unilaterally, so to speak. Even if there is only a handful of people who receive the communication, it has proved its presence.

I do not want to labour the parallel. When such confrontations arise, can we really doubt whose testimony reflects a truth?

Nor is the underlying situation changed even if we consider *groups* of critics arguing about *groups* of works. The moment we interpret the conflict in terms of pre-selected fields of communication, we come to understand it.

Pre-selected fields of communication

EX. 100

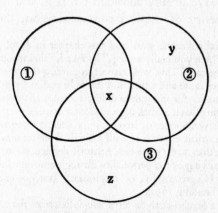

Only X is placed within all three fields of musical communication; consequently, only X understands all three works. By contrast, Y and Z are unfavourably placed; both lie outside two fields of communication. Moreover, they are mutually incapable of understanding one another's points of view. If Z claims that *3* is a masterpiece, Y might well regard this view as nonsense. Likewise, if Y claims that *2* is a masterpiece, Z could regard this view equally as nonsense. It is a sobering thought that the critic who maintains that a work is not a masterpiece, in flat contradiction to those who maintain that it is, is hearing things from the limited field of communication of a Y or a Z.[1]

Such "demarcation disputes" are illuminated for us the moment we consider them in the light of unconscious identification. A critic takes a particular stand in relation to music, and in relation to his fellow critics, not because he is free to do so but because he is not. His position has been unconsciously pre-selected for him, just as theirs has for them. "Demarcation disputes" are psychological phenomena and can, therefore, only be interpreted in psychological terms. A critic's positive musical response is symptomatic of libidinal release—which is the essence of the artistic experience[2]—and it results in pleasure. A negative response, on the other hand, is symptomatic of a libidinal block—and it results in "unpleasure".[3] For this reason, founded on strong psychological evidence, I take the view that a critic who loves a work, who finds pleasure in it, has *cathected*[4] with it and must, *ipso facto*, be glimpsing more of the truth about it than one who has not.

Insofar as I have already unfolded the first, and most important, half of my theory of musical communication, the moment has

---

[1] A close musical colleague who read this chapter in detail put the following objection to me. "Are you really saying," he asked, "that if someone *says* a work is great it *becomes* great?" This, with respect, is putting the question back to front, confusing as it does cause and effect, and the only reason I report it here is that I can see an opportunity for misunderstanding to arise. His question should really run: "Are you saying that if a work *is* great, someone will *say* it is great?" To which my simple reply is yes. Sooner or later mastery attracts recognition.

[2] To equate the artistic experience with a libidinal release may seem a novel act. It is, in fact, more than 2,000 years old. Aristotle defined the artistic experience as "catharsis"—a purifying of the personality through emotional discharge.

[3] Freud's term. He preferred it to "displeasure" (see, for example, *Beyond the Pleasure Principle*, London, 1950).

[4] "Cathexis" is a psycho-analytic term which describes the unconscious attachment of emotional bonds to objects and persons. Freud once described mental life as "the interplay of reciprocally urging and checking forces". The urging forces are "cathexes", and the checking forces are "anti-cathexes".

come to interrupt it in order to consider a simple objection. My diagnosis of the composer–listener relationship appears to be incomplete. To show why this is so, let me briefly recapitulate. After I had postulated the unconscious mechanism of identification as the "cause" of musical communication, and its absence as the "cause" of non-communication, it became imperative to ask what triggered this mechanism into activity. It will be recalled (p. 93) that I said this was accomplished by the unconscious libidinal stream engaged in its continual search for objects to which it might attach itself, thus achieving release from the listener's personality, lowering his psychic tension, giving him pleasure. But this is really a *petitio principii*. The question I begged, in fact, was why libido should become attached to *certain* works and not to *others*. What, in short, "causes" the "cause"? This is where the second half of my theory comes in. I should like to describe the concept as "moving historical backgrounds".

Moving historical backgrounds

"He's ripe for the madhouse", remarked Weber after hearing Beethoven's Seventh Symphony. We can only assume, as Charles Ives once observed in a different connection, that his "ears were on wrong". And this is no disrespect to Weber with whose evaluation posterity has so profoundly come to disagree. For I contend that our ears are "on wrong" for many works of genius that we are hearing for the first time; and, as we have seen, for certain kinds of listener listening to certain kinds of works, their ears are for ever locked in the wrong position. What you know, determines what you do not know.

A bird's-eye view of musical history reveals an intriguing phenomenon. It is becoming increasingly obvious that we no longer hear music as its contemporaries heard it. We have only to read accounts of the latest trends in music, at whatever stage in musical history they were introduced, to know that there is a difference between the way those trends sounded *then* and the way they sound *now*. Our historical background has moved. I regard this as the clearest proof of the long-range effects of unconscious assimilation. When Weber failed to identify with Beethoven's Seventh Symphony, he not only disclosed something about himself: he disclosed something about Beethoven, too. At the same time, both disclosed something about musical criticism. Whenever one musical mind repels another, the cause lies in their respective pasts. The past is where they both start from. Communication between them depends on the common terms of reference both have assimilated while growing up. Indeed, the only way new music can cross from one mind to another is by unconsciously "linking up" with the music both minds already know. Musical foregrounds are comprehended in terms of the common musical backgrounds across which they unfold; that is to say, where there is no common background, incomprehension ensues. In this respect, the evolution of composition has yielded an interesting by-product: a rising norm of foreground tension. Composers are forced to keep raising foreground tension *because listeners keep lowering it*. Backgrounds eventually swallow foregrounds; music evolves to survive. History shows that foreground tension is "killed" by increasing familiarity. The composer, like Alice, must run very hard indeed in order to stay still. The psychological fate of all musical progress is the same. Each new generation of listeners has the same uneasy time of it with each new generation of composers. Yet the moment listeners have begun to assimilate the new, have incorporated it into their own musical backgrounds, it is drained of its tension; and the reason is that it has now become an acceptable part of the listener's own musical personality. Where he cannot assimilate the new, the grinding friction between foreground and background ensures that his musical unconscious will take the only defensive measure open to it: he will reject it. Schoenberg summed it up in one of his famous aphorisms: "Only the developing composer can compose for the developing listener".

But we not only hear the new against a background of the old: we also hear the old against a background of the new, a contingency against which no composer can insure himself. Any consideration of moving historical backgrounds leads us straight to a phenomenon of *communicative progression and regression*. We assimilate nothing without subtly shifting the balance of our musical point of view. Our ears may be "on wrong" retrospectively as well as prospectively.

Let me be more specific. The following diagram (for whose seeming pedantry I apologise in advance; I know of no better way of making more immediate what is a complex situation) typifies a progressing and regressing foreground–background relationship. Shaded circles depict listeners; white circles depict works.

EX. 101

Non-comprehension, partial comprehension; total comprehension; partial incomprehension. It is a familiar tale, this swing in critical attitudes, endlessly repeated throughout musical history. My illustrations summarise the psychological fate of a work across several generations. At first (Fig. (a)) it remains uncomprehended; it may have stood out too boldly for comfort against the musical background of its own time and been rejected. The next two stages in its career (Figs. (b) and (c)) show a gradual, then total, acceptance of it as the gap between foreground and background closes, and intense identification becomes possible. The final stage (Fig. (d)) shows a partial loss of access to the work for the background against which it is played has shifted yet again. This time, it is heard by a distant generation against a future background, a background as yet uncomposed and unimagined when the composer lived and worked.

Listeners will always reach out to composers; but however intensely they identify with them, it is the fate of a composer to be heard more clearly at certain times than at others. There is a sense in which a composer has to vie with other composers for the ears of his listeners. His lines of communication, in consequence, become posthumously modified; but this is a process which, as we have seen, can work for him as well as against him.

We "distort" the present, then, through our experience of the past, just as we "distort" the past through our experience of the present. This is a fundamental aesthetic phenomenon which scholars, historians, musicologists—all those whose primary concern is the "preservation" of the music of the past—have unwittingly made highly topical. "A proper conception of musical history involves 'historical listening'—listening, that is to say, with the ears of another age and with all subsequent music banished from the mind."[1]

[1] *An Introduction to Musical History*, J. A. Westrup, p. 152, London, 1955.

It is fortunate—to judge by some of history's bewildered reactions—that we do not hear music "with the ears of another age". We should understand precious little of it if we did. The notion that the musician is a time-traveller, that he can forsake his own background, move across history, and hear music with the immediacy of a contemporary, ignores some hard facts. It is one of the great lessons of depth psychology that you can "banish" nothing from the mind.[1] Our ears are "on wrong" willy-nilly. No experience is too transient not to leave its indelible impression on our minds, later to return as an active conditioner of each subsequent experience.

I should like to try to sharpen the concept of historical backgrounds. What follows is not a digression. It will quickly be seen to be relevant.

For many years, Fritz Kreisler regularly incorporated in his recitals "newly-discovered" works which, he claimed, were by eighteenth-century composers. So popular did these pieces become (he played them regularly as encore items) that they were eventually published in a series called "Classical Manuscripts". Vivaldi, Tartini, Boccherini and Couperin were among the "composers" included. Then, in 1935, Kreisler announced to the Press that these "classical" works were, in fact, his own compositions. There was a considerable furore at the time, particularly among the critics who were forced into the embarrassing position of having to do some quick re-evaluating. Inevitably, these pieces which critics had formerly regarded as finds of great musical interest were now called "worthless", "rubbishy", "pastiche", etc.

My point is not that music critics are fallible. There are deeper considerations here. Consider a simple question. Why should our attitude to music change once it has been established that it is no longer "authentic"? The work remains exactly the same as before. Its intrinsic qualities are not changed one jot by the news that it is the work of someone else. Before attempting an explanation, let me give one or two more instances of hoaxes that have led to a *volte-face* in the world of criticism.

During the Promenade Concerts season of 1929 Sir Henry Wood

[1] There are no "authentic" performances of old music because there are no longer any "authentic" listeners. Everybody listens to the past with corrupted ears.

conducted the first performance of an orchestral transcription of Bach's well-known Toccata and Fugue in D minor by Paul Klenovsky. Its success was instantaneous. In 1934 the Oxford University Press expressed interest in publishing the transcription and Sir Henry was asked for Klenovsky's address. He then had to admit that he himself was "Klenovsky" (the name was that of a promising pupil of Glazunov's who had died young) and that he had adopted the pseudonym simply because certain purist critics had on previous occasions severely criticised other orchestrations by him. "Klenovsky", he thought, might make a better orchestrator. And so it proved. This time, the critics had been unanimous in their praise.

In 1911 Ravel composed his set of piano pieces *Valses Nobles et Sentimentales*. They were first performed at a concert given by the Société Musicale Indépendante at which the authorship of all new compositions on the programme was kept secret. Ravel's friends were unanimous in condemning the work until they realised that he himself had written it.

Again, let me stress that my point is not the fallibility of music critics. Why should our reactions to music depend upon whether we know it to be by a great composer or by a nonentity? The music remains unaltered. It is only a mere bit of information about it, a name, which is different.

The fact is, as we have seen, our aesthetic experience of music does not consist only of what we hear. It consists of what we do not hear, too. On the one hand, there is the work itself—the "primary" source. On the other, there are all the works by the same composer (and many others historically related to him)—the "secondary" source. What we already know of a composer's music conditions the way in which we react to something unfamiliar by him. The aesthetic experience is always compounded of this interplay between the "primary" appreciation field and the "secondary" appreciation field.[1] As soon as we are told that a work is by (say)

[1] To anyone familiar with Calvocoressi's theory of criticism* it may appear that I have arrived at the same conclusions as him—albeit by a very different route. The last two of his three "categories" of critical perception (viz. "direct data"—by which he meant the work under consideration, and "indirect data"—by which he meant accessory information contained in works by the same composer) appear to be identical with what I call the "primary field" and the "secondary field". In fact, our two theories are poles apart. Calvocoressi's "direct data" and "indirect

Beethoven, this one piece of information is enough to trigger into activity a "secondary" field which looms large behind the work itself, the "primary" field, and which colours it—albeit on an unconscious level. But suppose that we later learn that the work is not by Beethoven at all, that it is by a nonentity. Then its links with the "secondary" field are severed. We listen to it in a different "frame of mind". And this, too, is the whole case against anonymity. Anonymity snaps the connection between these two fields, a connection upon which complete musical understanding vitally depends. The "innocent ear" is a fiction. It is based upon the absurd notion that what we hear now can in some way be isolated from past experience. There is no such thing as "pure" perception. All ears are "guilty". Understanding infiltrates music by virtue of other music we unconsciously relate to it. Understanding is memory.

The following diagram illustrates the situation.

EX. 102

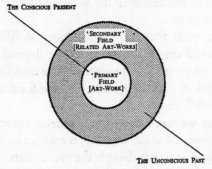

THE CONSCIOUS PRESENT

'SECONDARY' FIELD [RELATED ART-WORKS]

'PRIMARY' FIELD [ART-WORK]

THE UNCONSCIOUS PAST

All hoaxers go wrong in ignoring this dual aspect of the aesthetic experience. They imagine that aesthetic reactions are based exclusively on the observed work of art, and that when a listener rhapsodises over a work later shown to be a fake, he exposes himself as a fool. It is the hoaxer who is the real fool, however. He overlooks that vast, pre-existent reservoir of positive responses which all of us gradually acquire and then unconsciously project on to new

---

data" describe the *conscious* sources from which evidence necessary to formulate value-judgements is derived. By contrast, my "primary field" and "secondary field" describe the *unconscious relationship* in which one work stands to another and out of which emerges our intuitive attitude towards it.

* *The Principles and Methods of Music Criticism*, London, 1923. See the excellent synopsis of his ideas in "Music Criticism", Harvard Dictionary of Music.

works by great composers. What you know influences what you do not know. Without this unconscious tendency, no hoax would be possible. For the hoaxer creeps in under its cover and exploits it. He robs a work of its true background and fabricates a false one. The listener is easy game; he takes music on trust. The hoaxer does not; his attitude is essentially that of the perverted lawyer who regards everybody as guilty until proved innocent. But musical criticism never has, and never can operate on such a principle.

Far from representing a detour, a careful consideration of what it is that constitutes a hoax and how exactly it differs from what constitutes "honest" musical communication seems, to me, to be an ideal method of disclosing the presence of historical backgrounds, and their function. A historical background can push a listener towards a work, or it can pull him away from one. It is an indispensable factor in fixing the view from which the listener observes the composer. No theory of criticism can afford to neglect it.

But what has it to do with the first part of our theory, that of "unconscious identification"?

A Synthesis

At first sight, I appear to have changed horses in mid-stream. The concept of "moving historical backgrounds" seems to have little to do with that of "unconscious identification"—an aspect of our theory which we apparently abandoned some pages ago. Indeed, these two concepts give the impression of being somewhat contradictory. For if it is historical backgrounds which determine whether or not music shall communicate, why postulate unconscious identification at all? To put the contradiction another way: Was it not a mistake to have proposed unconscious identification as the *key* to our theory of musical communication in view of the crucial role played by historical backgrounds?

I do not think it was a mistake. Nor do I think there is any contradiction in our theory. What I have called the listener's "historical background" is nothing less than the *sum total of all the music he has previously identified with*. He has no "historical background" unless and until he "identifies", for this is his only means of acquiring one. The two "conflicting" concepts are, in fact, different sides of the same coin. It is by a continual process of unconscious identification, particularly in his formative years, that the musician gradually builds up the historical backgrounds against which he listens—or composes. Historical backgrounds, then, are synonymous with his musical psychology—are *symptoms* of it. That is why I argue that *musical* history (as opposed to musical *history*) is an internal phenomenon. Musical history, unlike the history of most other subject, is not "out there". We get to know music by stealing it from history, so to speak, by making it a part of us, by internalising it. Then, it is no longer a true historical phenomenon at all; it is a psychological one. So much for the so-called "pressures" of musical history; they do not exist; all such pressure is psychological. Admittedly, there *is* a sense in which musical history can remain truly historical, not become truly psychological, and that is when it is history which is uncomprehended. Needless to add, this is not the kind of history I am discussing. When musical history is truly known to us, when we have assimilated it into our musical personality, then and only then does it exercise any "pressure"; and by that time it has ceased to be "history" and has become instead a dynamic part of our musical unconscious. Again, the "pressure of environment" to which music and musicians supposedly succumb has no claim on a theory of musical criticism. Time and again, musical developments which were first thought to have been formed by "pressure of environment", turn out to have been a latent part of those musical developments from the start. Music makes history; history does not make music. Indeed, what the historian, combing music's environment for facts, calls a "cause" often emerges *after* the event that this "cause" is supposed to have brought about—like the gun in a badly managed stage-production which goes off after the villain has already dropped dead.[1]

[1] This assertion, I think, is likely to lead to a demand for detailed substantiation. I will give two brief examples which may help to clarify my point of view.

Take Sébastien Érard's invention of the "double-escapement" which he introduced into his pianos in 1821. This device makes possible the most rapid reiteration of single notes. Historians often regard the innovation as the cause of the great increase in virtuosic note-repetitions in romantic piano music. A piece like Liszt's *La Campanella* (1838), for instance, would be impossible to play without Érard's invention. In fact, the introduction of the double-escapement *had* to come because there was a creative *need* for it. Keyboard music, particularly Beethoven's, was becoming increasingly awkward. It was creative, musical pressure which pushed aside the mechanical limitations of the early piano and resulted in this particular break-through. Music made history.

The other example is equally curious. It has been widely assumed among his-

All influence, cultural or otherwise in T. S. Eliot's phrase, "intro-duce one to oneself".[1] Psychologically, "influence" is largely what you need to be influenced by in order to develop. It is a deeply mysterious process, but one to which everybody can testify. It is equally true of composers and listeners alike. When a composer "influences" a listener he is doing nothing less than revealing a part of that listener's own musical personality to him. And where do the musical principles, the principles I formulated in Part Two, fit into the psychological theory I have just outlined? The answer is that they emerge as *rationalisations*[2] from within the framework of our positive responses towards composers and their works. Theory, as I said before, follows practice. The proper philosophical position for all principles in art criticism, subordinate though it is, I believe to exist well and truly after the event.

My account of these principles, and of the psychological back-ground from which they derive, is hardly complete. In this little volume, my immediate purpose has been to point towards a direc-tion in which a theory of criticism might more fully be unfolded. Its further development I hope to set out in a future book.

---

torians that the emergence of the sixteenth-century *antiphonal* style in the works of Willaert and the two Gabrieli's was directly influenced by the architecture of St Mark's Cathedral, Venice, which first prompted these composers to employ con-trasting "echo" effects—a musical characteristic long associated with this School. But deeper acquaintance with the music of earlier periods shows that the "outer" influence of St Mark's architecture had nothing to do with the emergence of the *antiphonal* style which led an "inner" musical existence long before the "St Mark's" group appeared.

[1] *To Criticise the Critic*, p. 126, London, 1965.
[2] I use the term *rationalisation* to mean "intellectualisation"—a process of moving from the intuitive to the conceptual.

CONCLUSIONS

MY book is not an attack against criticism; it is a defence of criticism. Even so, the theory it unfolds will almost certainly not remain unchallenged. The twofold conclusion towards which it drives is too stark for that.

First: the practice of criticism is destined to remain at the litmus-paper stage. Critics take a dip into music and we see what colour they turn. That, basically, is all critical practice is about. Second: the practice of criticism is really a solution in search of a problem. How a critic reacts is already pre-determined by deep-rooted musical and psychological force. That, basically, is all critical theory is about.

How does this constitute a "defence" of criticism?—in view of the nature of my theory the term seems almost ironical. I think that we do criticism a great disservice by emphasising its intellectual aspects. An act of criticism is not an act of intelligence: it is an act of intuition. The intellect is there only to move in after the intuitive event, to explain it. It would make no difference to a critical reaction if it did not move in at all. Litmus-paper still changes colour even when we are not interested in knowing why. Good critics, then, are sleepwalkers; this tends to keep them in close touch with composers who, as we have seen, do quite a lot of sleepwalking of their own. It is the wide-awake intellect which has to grope in the dark and which stumbles over obstacles that the sleepwalking critic easily avoids.

For the rest, there is one, indispensable symptom without which both the theory and practice of criticism remain sterile. Koussevitzky was once rehearsing Berlioz's Fantastic Symphony. During the interval a listener approached him and remarked that there was a great deal of bombast in the score. Koussevitzky looked pained and said: "Even if it is so, I don't want to discuss it. I must not think of defects when I play the music." Like performance, criticism should proceed on a basis of positive, intuitive involvement; paradoxically, it leads to the truth about music far more quickly than a negative search for defects. This, incidentally, is the unanswerable case against "objective" criticism which, being psychologically impossible, is correspondingly truthless. How do you criticise music you insist on holding at arms' length? Until you have embraced it, assimilated it, there is nothing to criticise; but once you have, your "objectivity" has vanished. The dying echoes of the great "objective–subjective" debate can, as a matter of fact, still be heard today in the drawing-rooms of the musical intelligentsia. They need not detain us, however.

All critical conflict, by definition, points in two or more directions simultaneously. What we want to know is in which direction does the truth suffer least—the most any criticism may hope to achieve? I think that criticism which instinctively leaps to the defence *when confronted by attack*, is in a far stronger psychological position than criticism which leaps to the attack *when confronted by defence*. A critic functions most truly, I believe, when he plays the role of counsel for the defence. If he finds himself out of sympathy with the evidence he ought not to accept the case. I am by no means the first musician to think thus about criticism, although I may well be the first to want to base a theory of aesthetics on that belief.

BIBLIOGRAPHY

This bibliography consists solely of those books which have been useful to me in writing my own.

Apel, Willi, "Musical Criticism" (article: *Harvard Dictionary of Music*), London, 1951.

Bell, Clive, *Art*, London, 1900.

Blom, Eric, *The Limitations of Music*, London, 1928.

Busoni, Ferruccio, *The Essence of Music*, London, 1957.

Calvocoressi, M. D., *Principles and Methods of Musical Criticism*, London, 1923. 2nd enlarged ed. Oxford, 1931.

Cooke, Deryck, *The Language of Music*, London, 1959.

Cooper, Grosvenor, and Meyer, Leonard, *The Rhythmic Structure of Music*, Chicago, 1960.

Dean, Winton, "Criticism" (article: *Grove V*), London, 1955.

Dorian, Frederick, *The Musical Workshop*, London, 1947.

Durant, Will, *Outlines of Philosophy*, London, 1947.

Ehrenzweig, Anton, *The Psycho-analysis of Artistic Vision and Hearing*, London, 1953.

Eliot, T. S. *To Criticize the Critic*, London, 1965.

Forster, E. M., "The Raison d'être of Criticism in the Arts" (Symposium: *Two Cheers for Democracy*), London, 1951.

Freud, Anna, *The Ego and the Mechanisms of Defence*, London, 1961.

Freud, Sigmund, *The Interpretation of Dreams*, Vienna, 1899.
  Introductory Lectures in Psycho-analysis, London, 1922.
  Leonardo da Vinci, London, 1948.
  Group Psychology, London, 1922.

Fry, Roger, "The Artist and Psycho-analysis" (*Hogarth Essay*), London, 1924.
  "An Essay in Aesthetics" (from *Vision and Design*), London, 1923.

Hadow, Sir Henry, *Studies in Modern Music* (First and Second Series), London, 1894.

Hindemith, Paul, *A Composer's World*, Harvard, 1952.

Joad, C. E. M., *Guide to Philosophy*, London, 1948.

Keller, Hans, "Mozart's Chamber Music" (*The Mozart Companion*) eds. Donald Mitchell and Robbins Landon, London, 1956.

and Cosman, Milein, *Stravinsky in Rehearsal*, London, 1962.

Köhler, W., *Gestalt Psychology*, 1930.

Langer, Susanne, *Problems of Art*, London, 1957.

Mauron, C., "Aesthetics and Psychology" (*Hogarth Essay*), London, 1935.

"The Nature of Beauty in Art and Literature" (*Hogarth Essay*), London, 1927.

Meyer, Leonard, *Emotion and Meaning in Music*, Chicago, 1956.

Newman, Ernest, *A Musical Critic's Holiday*, London, 1925.

From The World of Music, London, 1956.

Read, Sir Herbert, *The Meaning of Art*, London, 1931.

Révész, G., *Introduction to the Psychology of Music*, London, 1953.

Russell, Bertrand, *History of Western Philosophy*, London, 1946.

Scholes, Percy, "Criticism of Music" (article: *Oxford Companion to Music*), 9th edn, London, 1955.

Schoenberg, Arnold, "Criteria for the Evaluation of Music" (essay: *Style and Idea*), London, 1951.

Stravinsky, Igor, *The Poetics of Music*,

and Craft, Robert, *Conversations with Igor Stravinsky*, London, 1959.

Memories and Commentaries, London, 1960.

Expositions and Developments, London, 1962.

Tovey, Sir Donald, *Essays in Musical Analysis* (Vols. 1-6), London, 1935-39.

The Integrity of Music, London, 1914.

Walker, Alan, *A Study in Musical Analysis*, London, 1962.

"Chopin and Musical Structure" (*Frédéric Chopin*, ed. Alan Walker), London, 1966.

INDEX

ABELL, Arthur, 88
A priori principles, nature of, 3–4, 81–2
Analysis, 28
Aristotle, 5, 96
Auer, Leopold, 24
"Authentic" performance, 100

Bach, J. S.
  Vivaldi arrangements, 69–71
  Wohltemperiertes Clavier, 17
  See Index to Music Examples
Beethoven, Ludwig van, xi, 15–16, 35,
  49, 57
  Sketch Books, 65–7
  talking about the creative process,
  38–9
  See Index to Music Examples
Berlioz, Hector
  Fantastic Symphony, 43, 86, 107
Blacher, Boris, 34
Boccherini, Luigi, 100
Borodin
  Prince Igor, 91
Brahms, Johannes, 14–15, 34, 37, 50,
  64, 77, 93
  talking about the creative process, 88
  See Index to Music Examples
Brodsky, Adolf, 24
Buridan, 82

Calvocoressi, M. D., xii, 101–2
Carner, Mosco, 79

Catharsis, 96
Cathexis, 96
Chopin, Frédéric, 18–19, 43, 49–50, 86
  See Index to Music Examples
Clementi, Muzio, 15
Cooke, Deryck, 58
Content (*see* Form)
Copland, Aaron, 64
  talking about the creative process, 88
Cosman, Milein, 90
Couperin, François, 23, 100
  L'art de toucher le clavecin, 23
Craft, Robert, 5, 17
Creative determinism, 4–7
Criticism
  "confrontations", 94–7
  definition of, 5
  means *versus* ends, 8
  methods of comparison, 7–8
  music as communication, 9
  nature of, xii
  objective *versus* subjective, 107
  practice *versus* theory, xi
  principles of, (*see* principles)
Curzon, Clifford, 17

Debussy, Claude, 13–14, 15
  letter to Jacques Durand, 64–5
  Nocturnes, 26
  talking about Satie, 73
  See Index to Music Examples
Delius, Frederick 15

Demuth, Norman, 18
Deutsch, Otto, 34, 85, 86
Diabelli, 57
Dietrich, Albert, 50
   See Index to Music Examples
dis-unity, 50–2
Dvorak, Antonin, 64

Einstein, Alfred, 34, 69
Elgar, Sir Edward, 8, 15, 71
   See Index to Music Examples
Eliot, T. S., 105
Érard, Sébastien, 104
Eroica Symphony, xii, 74, 91
Experimental masterpieces, 8

"Fingerprints" in music, 35
Form (*see* Content)
Freud, 96
   Interpretation of Dreams, 90
   origin of artistic impulse, 92–3

Gabrielis, Giovanni and Andrea, 105
Gershwin, George, 35
Gestalt psychology, 5
Glazunov's memory, 91
Goethe, 85, 86
Grieg, Edvard, 76
   See Index to Music Examples

Hadow, Sir Henry, xii
Handel
   Messiah, 86
Haydn
   The Creation, 87
Hindemith, Paul, 17, 73
   writing about unity, 39
Historical Backgrounds, 97–100
Hoaxes, 100–1
Huettenbrenner, Joseph, 86

Ibert, Jacques
   Divertissement, 50
Ives, Charles, 97

Joachim, Joseph, 50
Joad, C. E. M., 6

Keller, Hans, 14, 90
Klenovsky, Paul, 101

Koussevitzky, Sergei, 107
Kreisler, Fritz, 100

Latham, Peter, 64
Laughter music, 50
Law of parsimony, 64
Libido, 91–3, 97
Listener–composer relationship, 89–96,
   97–9
Liszt, Franz, 34, 57
   La Campanella, 104
   Paganini Studies, 71–2
   Transcendental Studies, 67–8
   See Index to Music Examples
Löhn, Fritz, 84–5

Mahler, Gustav, 57
   orchestration of Schumann sym-
     phonies, 79–80
   Symphony of a Thousand, 84–5
Mahler Society, 57–8
Mann, William, 32
Mayerhofer, 85
Mendelssohn, Felix, 4
   letter to Marc-André Souchay, 4
   Songs without Words, 4
Mona Lisa, 91
Moscheles, Ignaz, 57
Mozart, Leopold, 23
Mozart, Wolfgang Amadeus, xi, 84
   A Musical Joke, 50
   Don Giovanni, 86
   Jupiter Symphony, 82
   See Index to Music Examples
Musical communication, 95–6
Mussorgsky, 78

Newman, Ernest, xii, 7, 10, 39, 74, 88
   A Musical Critic's Holiday, 10
   talking about form, 73
Nielsen, Carl, 15

Paer, Ferdinando
   Achilles, 65, 68
Paganini, Niccolò, 71–2
   La Campanella, 72
   Twenty-four Caprices, 72
   See Index to Music Examples
Palestrina, 35
Parthenon, 91
Plautus, 94

Pragmatism, 82
Principles
  Audibility, 75–81
  Co-extension between form and content,
    73–5
  Economy, 64–75
  Identity between idea and utterance, 65
  Identity between idea and medium, 13–
    26
  Thematic chronology, 52–64
  Unity of contrasts, 26–52

Rachmaninoff, Sergei, 34
Ravel, Maurice, 78, 101
  Concerto for the left hand, 17–18
  See Index to Music Examples
Rawsthorne, Alan, 73
Reik, Theodor, 84
Repression, 91
Respighi, Ottorino, 49
Reti, Rudolph, 35
Révész, G., 90
Rimsky-Korsakov, 91

Satie, Erik, 73
Schafer, Murray, 85
Schenker, Heinrich, 27
Schoenberg, Arnold, xi, 36, 55, 78–9,
  83–4, 91
  Erwartung, 86
  Jacob's Ladder, 87
  writing about unity, 38
  See Index to Music Examples
Schubert, Franz, 57, 34, 46
  Erlkönig, 85–6
  Overture in F major, 86
  See Index to Music Examples
Schumann, Robert, 34, 50
  Rhenish Symphony, 79–80
Scott, Marion, 35
Sibelius, Jan, 8
Spaun, Joseph von, 85

Stanford, Sir Charles, 26
Strauss, Richard, 65
Stravinsky, Igor, xi, 5, 16–17, 83–4, 93
  See Index to Music Examples
Sublimation, 91
Suk, Joseph, 64, 68

Tartini
  Devil's Trill Sonata, 83, 88
Tchaikovsky, Peter Ilyitch, 23–4, 28,
  39, 43, 51–2, 76–7, 93
  letter to Nadejda von Meck, 41
  See Index to Music Examples
Tovey, Sir Donald, 76

Unconscious creation, 83–8
  dream music, 83–4
Unconscious identification, 90
  memory, 91
Unity, 26–7
  dis-unity, 50–2
  nature of, 38, 39
Urlinie, 34

Vivaldi, Antonio, 69–71, 100
  See Index to Music Examples

Wagner, Richard, 35, 93, 88
  talking about the creation of
    Rhinegold, 87
  See Index to Music Examples
Walton, Sir William, 85
  See Index to Music Examples
Weber, Carl Maria, 97
Webern, Anton, 25
  See Index to Music Examples
Weingartner, Felix, 25
Westrup, Sir Jack, 99
Willaert, Adrian, 103
Wittgenstein, Paul, 17, 64
Wood, Sir Henry, 100–1
Wurmser, Leo, 65

INDEX TO MUSIC EXAMPLES

BACH, J. S.:
Concerto in A minor for four harpsichords, 70

BEETHOVEN:
Symphonies
No. 3 in E flat major (*Eroica*), 66
No. 5 in C minor, 55–6, 66
No. 8 in F major, 45–9, 76
Concertos
Violin Concerto in D major, 16
Sonatas
Op. 13 (*Pathétique*), 52–4
Op. 106 (*Hammerklavier*), 24
Piano Trio in C minor (Op. 1), 78

BRAHMS:
Symphonies
No. 1 in C minor, 77
No. 2 in D major, 36–8
No. 3 in F major, 49
Quartets
in A minor, 14
Sonatas
"F.A.E." sonata movement, for violin and piano, 50

CHOPIN:
Polonaise in A flat major (Op. 53), 19
Prelude in C sharp minor (Op. 28), 75
Scherzo in C sharp minor, 18

DEBUSSY:
String Quartet in G minor, 13–14

DIETRICH:
"F.A.E." sonata movement for violin and piano, 50

ELGAR:
Violin Concerto in B minor, 29

GRIEG:
Piano Concerto in A minor, 81

LISZT:
Paganini Study (No. 2) in E flat major, 71–2
Transcendental Study (No. 8) in C minor (*Wilde jagd*), 68

MAHLER:
Re-orchestration of Schumann's *Rhenish* Symphony, 80

MOZART:
Piano Conerto in C minor (K. 491), 27–8
Piano Quartet in G minor (K. 478), 29–30
Piano Sonata in F major (K. 332), 60–2

PAGANINI:
Caprice in E flat major for unaccompanied violin, 71–2

RAVEL:
Piano Concerto for the left hand, 18

SCHUBERT:
String Quintet in C major, 31–4, 58–9

SCHUMANN:
Rhenish Symphony, 79
"F.A.E." sonata movements for violin and piano, 50

STRAVINSKY:
L'Histoire du soldat, 84

TCHAIKOVSKY:
Symphonies
No. 4 in F minor, 28, 77
No. 5 in E minor, 40–44
Romeo and Juliet, 51

VIVALDI:
Concerto in B minor for four violins, 69

WAGNER:
Prelude to *Parsifal*, 20–22

WALTON:
Symphony no. 2, 85

WEBERN:
Piano Variations, (Op. 27), 25